DREAMLAND

All About
Human
Body
Encyclopedia

TRIVIA QUESTIONS AND ANSWERS

Concept by:
Anuj Chawla

Compiled by:
Lata Seth

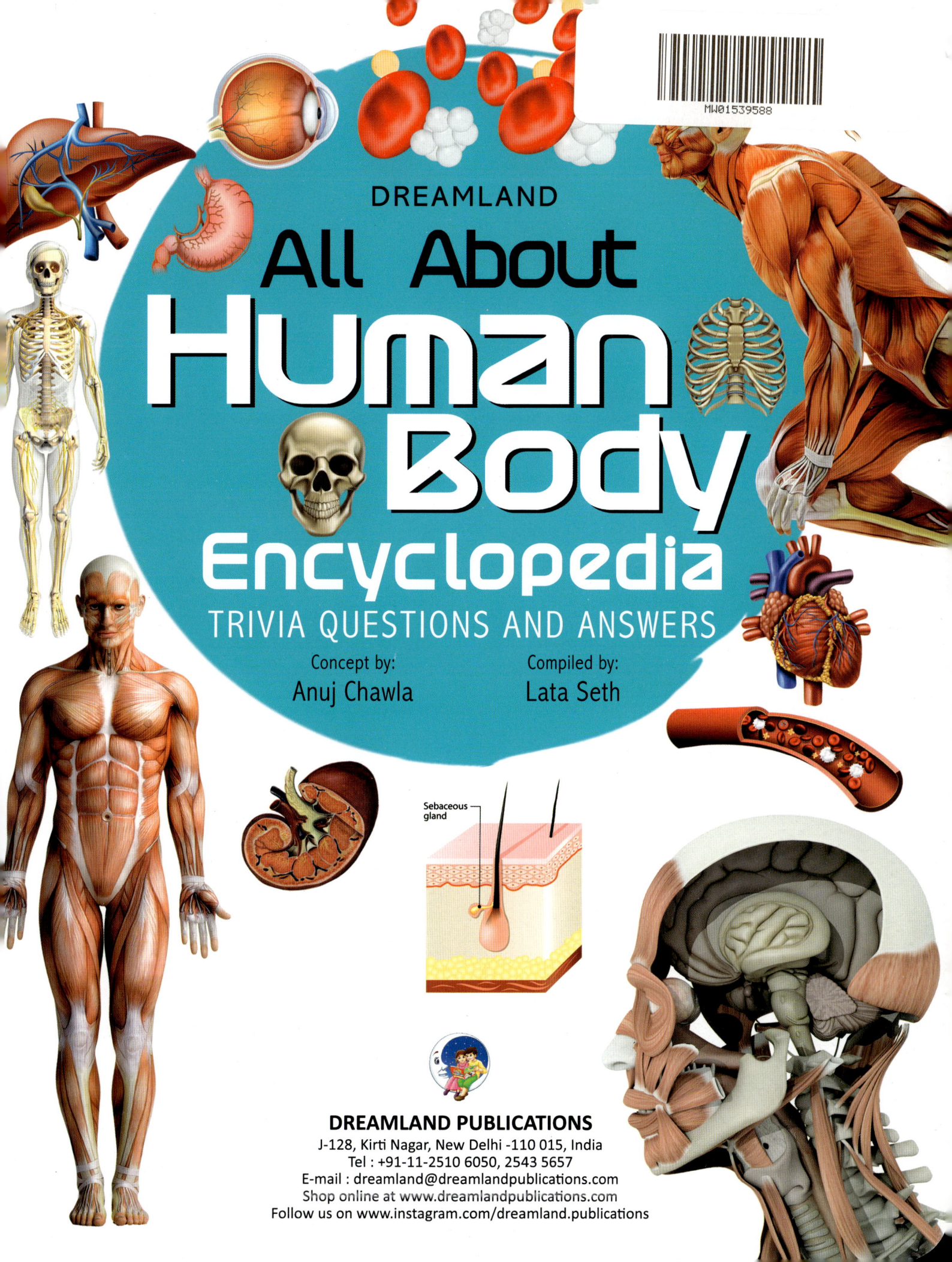

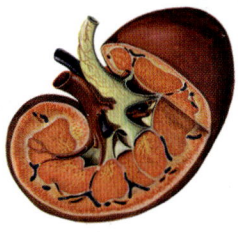

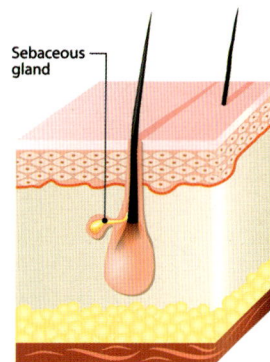

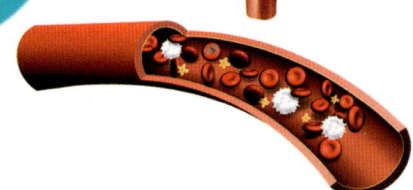

Sebaceous
gland

DREAMLAND PUBLICATIONS

J-128, Kirti Nagar, New Delhi -110 015, India
Tel : +91-11-2510 6050, 2543 5657
E-mail : dreamland@dreamlandpublications.com
Shop online at www.dreamlandpublications.com
Follow us on www.instagram.com/dreamland.publications

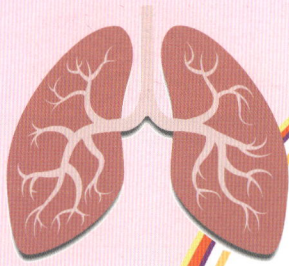

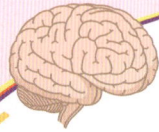

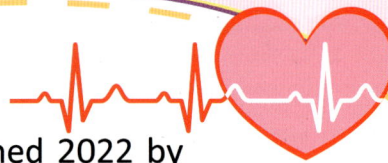

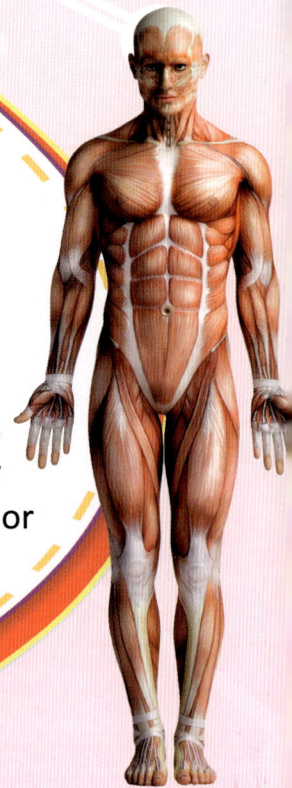

Published 2022 by

DREAMLAND PUBLICATIONS

J-128, Kirti Nagar, New Delhi - 110 015, India

Tel : +91-11-2510 6050, 2543 5657

E-mail : dreamland@dreamlandpublications.com

www.dreamlandpublications.com

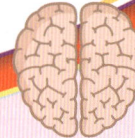

PREFACE

Children are born eager to learn. Curious by nature, they want to explore, discover, and figure things out. As such many questions come into their mind for which they seek answers.

Keeping in view their curiosity, Dreamland Publications has endeavoured to come up with "All About Encyclopedia Series" — a set of seven books with detailed, lively answers to many fascinating questions that young readers ask about the world around them.

This series covers subject areas such as the Animal Kingdom, Science and Technology, Space, Around the world, Human body, Nature and Amazing Places. Using a child-friendly format each question is clearly answered and fantastic images help explain things further.

This is a perfect series for young readers. We are sure that this series will be welcomed by the children, parents, and teachers alike.

WHAT DO YOU CALL THE STUDY OF THE HUMAN BODY?

The human body has two ways to study and research — anatomy and physiology. Anatomy is the study of the structure and relationship between body parts. Physiology is the study of the function of body parts and the body as a whole. Anatomy focuses on the description of form, or how body structures at different levels look. Physiology focuses on function, or how structures at different levels work.

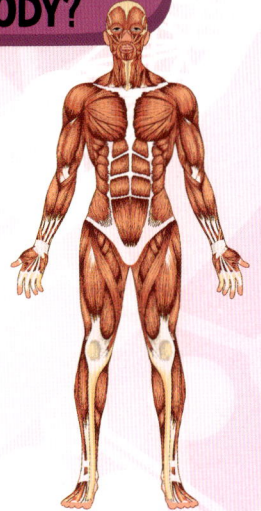

WHY DOES THE SENSE OF SMELL IN HUMANS DIMINISH AS THEY AGE?

The sense of smell decreases in humans as they grow older. About the time people are 70 years old, the sense of smell decreases, due to loss of nerve endings, or less mucous produced in the nose. This can prevent people from being able to fully taste the food, making them lose their appetite. It can be restored by using steroid nasal sprays or drops.

WHAT ARE AMINO ACIDS?

Amino acids are the building blocks of life. After proteins have been digested, the amino acids remain. They break down food, help the body to grow, and repair body tissue. Amino acids can also be used as a source of energy. The essential or standard amino acids only come from food. Non-essential amino acids are produced by the body, while Conditional amino acids are needed by us in times of sickness.

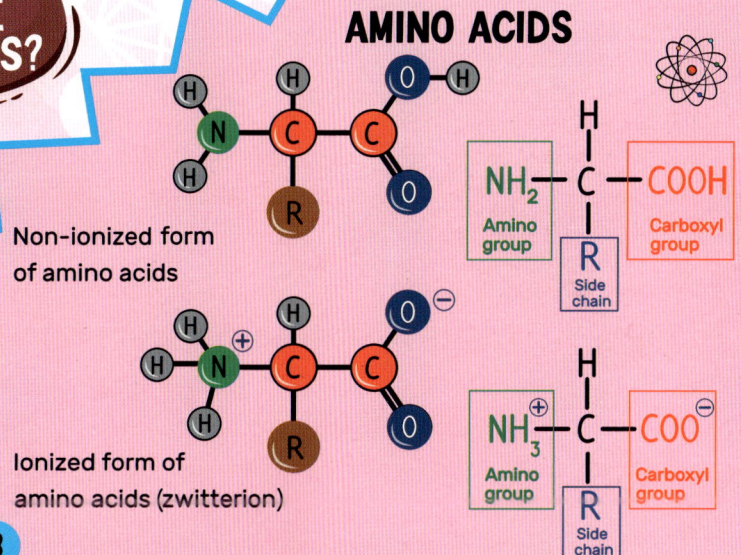

AMINO ACIDS

Non-ionized form of amino acids

Ionized form of amino acids (zwitterion)

NH_2 — Amino group

C

H

R Side chain

$COOH$ Carboxyl group

$NH_3^{\oplus}$ — Amino group

C

H

R Side chain

$COO^{\ominus}$ Carboxyl group

WHAT DOES OLFACTORY HAVE TO DO WITH?

Olfactory is the sense of smell, which helps us to detect pleasant or unpleasant odours. It is olfaction that helps us to distinguish between various odours which, in turn, helps in creating newer and delicious food recipes! Perfume creators, or oenologists, can differentiate between thousands of odours, as do wine tasters!

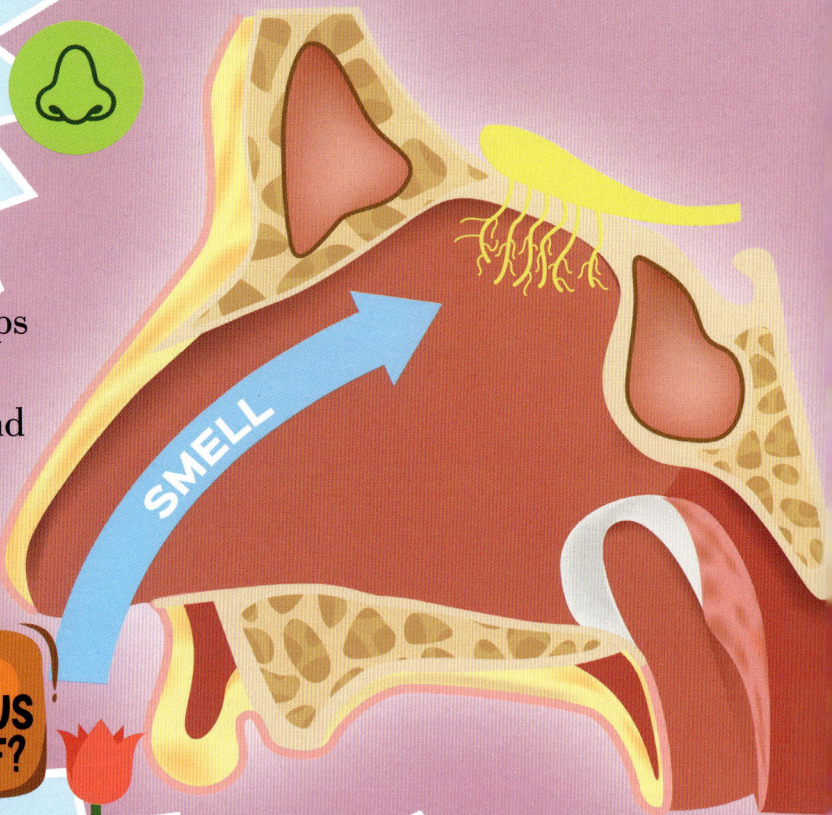

SMELL

WHAT IS OUR CENTRAL NERVOUS SYSTEM MADE OF?

BRAIN

SPINAL CORD

CNS CENTRAL NERVOUS SYSTEM

Our central nervous system (CNS) comprises the brain and spinal cord. Our brain integrates most of the sensory information and coordinates body function. The complex functions of thinking and feeling also, are carried out by different parts of the brain. The spinal cord serves as the conduit for signals, which are exchanged between the brain and other body parts.

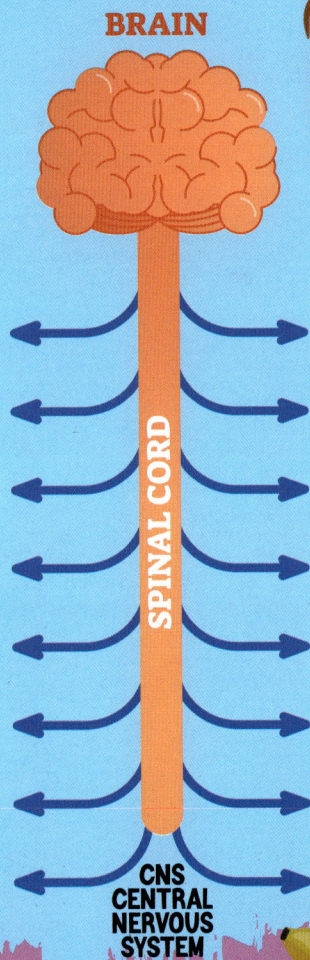

WHAT GIVES US ENERGY?

Food provides us energy in the form of calories, used by the body in every activity. Each gram of carbohydrates (carbs) and proteins gives us 4 calories, while every gram of fats gives us 9 calories. Complex carbs such as wheat pasta and brown rice; proteins such as chicken breasts or beans; and, fats such as nuts and seed oil are the best energy-giving foods. Besides, sugar provides energy to our muscles and brain.

HOW MUCH OF OUR BODY IS COMPOSED OF WATER?

An adult human body is composed of about 60% water! The brain and heart are made up of 73% water; our lungs are around 83% water; our muscles and kidneys contain 79% water; while, our skin is made up of 64% water. Our bones, too, though strong, consist of 31% water!

WHICH IS THE HARDEST SUBSTANCE IN OUR BODY?

Enamel is the hardest substance in our body. It contains 96% of minerals, with hydroxyapatite, a crystalline calcium phosphate being the chief mineral. The rest is made up of water and organic material. Tooth enamel, the most mineralized substance, is a tissue. The dentine tissue is covered in enamel or the shiny, hard layer that we daily brush.

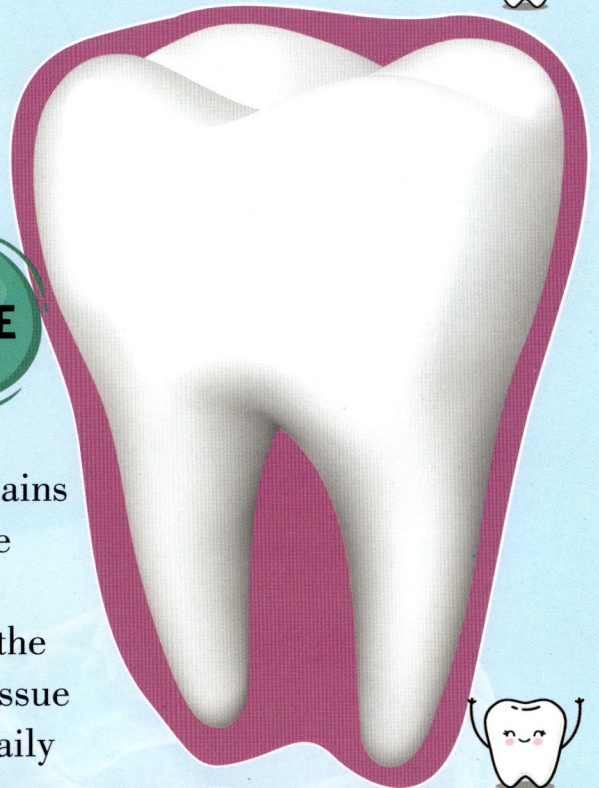

HOW DO OUR KIDNEYS DEAL WITH WASTE PRODUCTS?

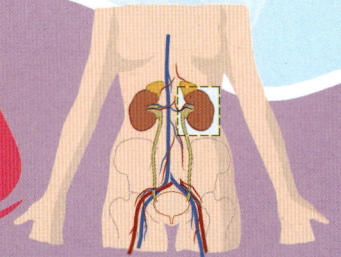

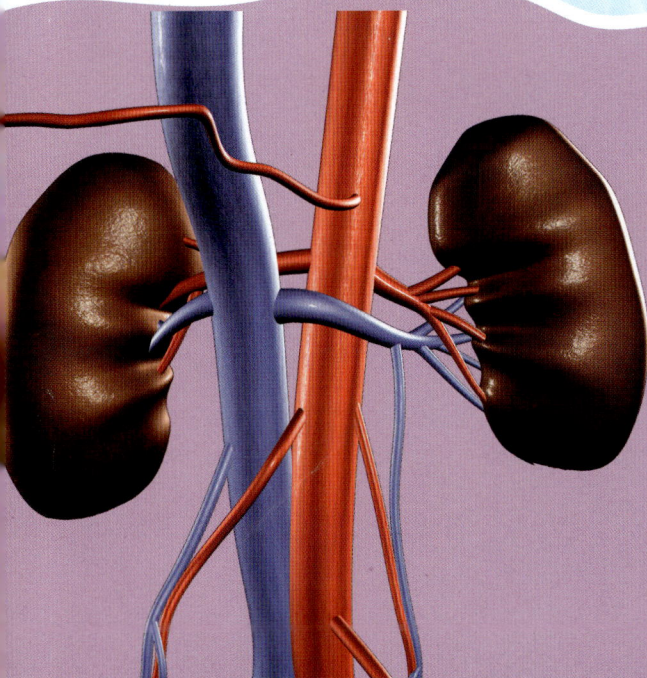

The human body has two kidneys that are bean-shaped organs, one on each side of the body, with each attached to a ureter or tube, which carries urine to the urinary bladder. The kidneys filter waste products from the blood while regulating the balance of salt and water in the body. Both, the kidney and urinary systems help in removing liquid waste from the blood, as urine.

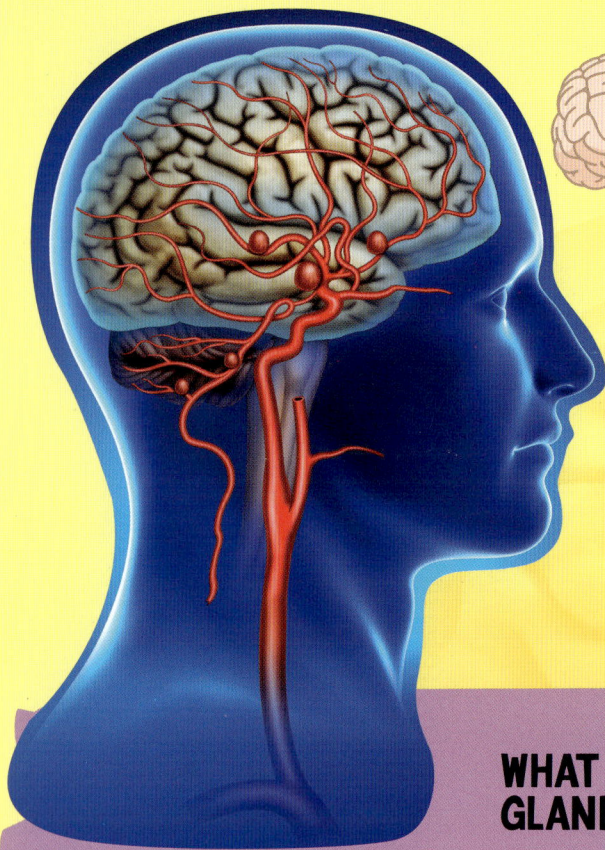

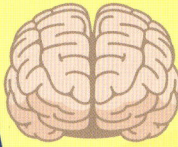

WHICH PART OF OUR BODY COORDINATES OUR VOLUNTARY MOVEMENTS?

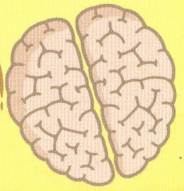

The hindbrain at the brain's lower back part, is one of the key parts of our central nervous system. It contains the pons, cerebellum, and medulla oblongata, besides many cranial nerves. The cerebellum coordinates voluntary muscle movements. Pons has many control areas to regulate eye and face movements; while the medulla controls heart and lung activity.

WHAT DOES THE THYROID GLAND SECRETE?

The thyroid gland secretes two main hormones, T3 or triiodothyronine, and T4 or thyroxine. These hormones regulate the body's heart rate, blood pressure, temperature, and metabolism, and depend on a proper supply of iodine. An under-functioning thyroid leads to Hypothyroidism, when somebody's functions slow down, causing fatigue, memory problems, and dry skin. An over-functioning thyroid leads to Hyperthyroidism, causing unintentional weight loss, rapid or irregular heartbeat, and increased rate of metabolism.

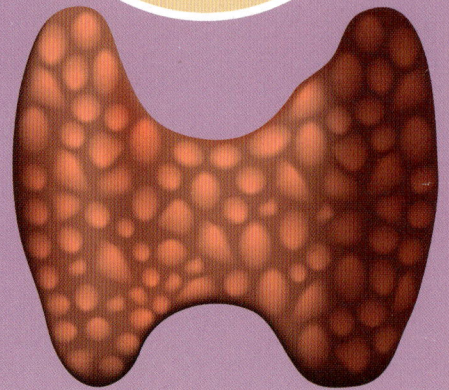

WHICH FOODS ARE RICH IN PROTEIN?

Proteins are very important; they help to make bones, muscles, skin, cartilage, and blood; build or repair body tissue; and, make hormones and enzymes. Foods rich in protein include eggs; fish, lean meat, and poultry; legumes and beans, especially lentils; dairy products including milk, cheese, and yogurt; nuts and seeds; and, soy products, like tofu.

HOW MANY SIDES IS OUR BRAIN DIVIDED INTO, AND WHAT DO THEY DO?

Our brain is a walnut-shaped organ, which is divided into two hemispheres or sides: left and right. The brain's left part controls logic and reasoning, helping people to do calculations and mathematics, besides being concerned with speech and language. The right part controls creativity and intuition and is concerned with artistic ability, as well as sight and hearing.

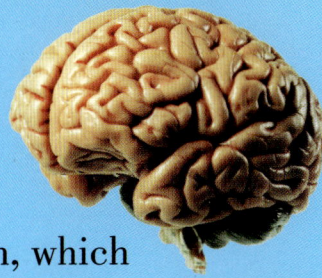

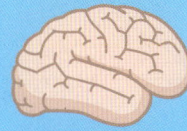

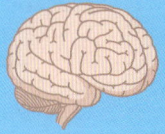

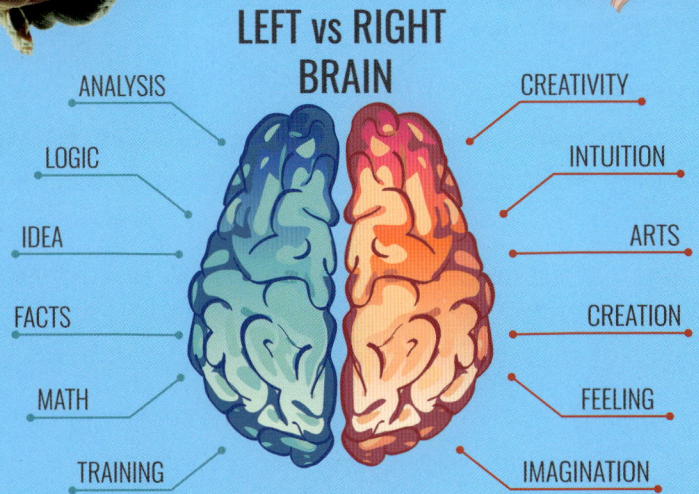

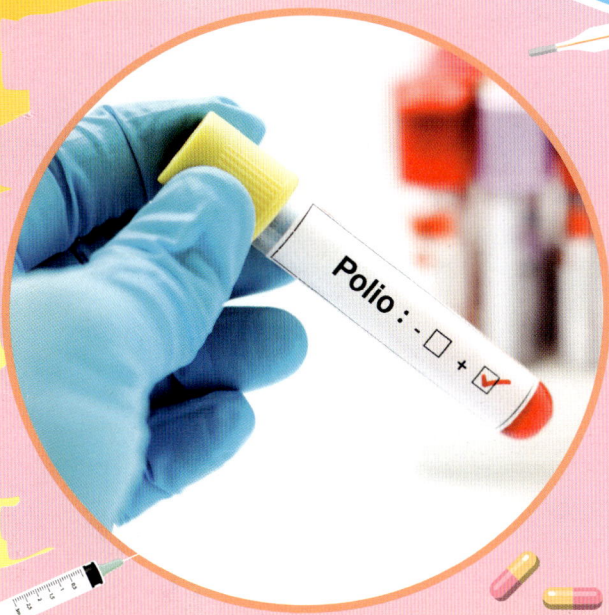

LEFT vs RIGHT BRAIN

ANALYSIS
LOGIC
IDEA
FACTS
MATH
TRAINING

CREATIVITY
INTUITION
ARTS
CREATION
FEELING
IMAGINATION

IS THERE ANYTHING THAT CAN PROTECT CHILDREN FROM POLIO?

Polio, or poliomyelitis, is an infectious disease, mostly affecting small children, which causes paralysis. It spreads by poliovirus, which enters through the mouth, and multiplies in the intestines. Polio cannot be cured but can be prevented. The first polio vaccine, made by Jonas Salk, was first used by him in 1954 to inject a group of school children, and commonly used in 1955. The oral polio drops, made by Albert Sabin, came into use in 1961, which have almost eradicated polio.

HOW CAN AN ILLNESS BE FOUND?

When someone falls ill, they go to a doctor who does a routine check-up, such as checking for fever, the pulse, and/or heart rate, and reaches a conclusion. This is a diagnosis. If need be, the doctor may ask the patient to take other tests, such as blood and/or urine test, an X-ray, etc., so that a 100% correct diagnosis is made, and treatment can begin.

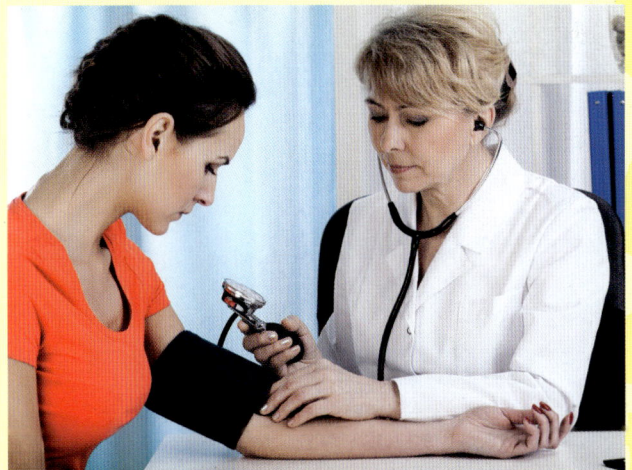

Trachea

Mycobacterium tuberculosis

Bronchi

WHAT CAUSES TUBERCULOSIS?

Tuberculosis or TB is caused by bacteria, mycobacterium tuberculosis, and mostly affects the lungs. It spreads through the air. When a person having TB coughs, sneezes, or spits, TB germs spread and can infect others. TB can infect other body parts, too, besides the lungs. It occurs in every part of the world and can happen to anyone. But it is a curable disease, and can also be prevented by taking proper care.

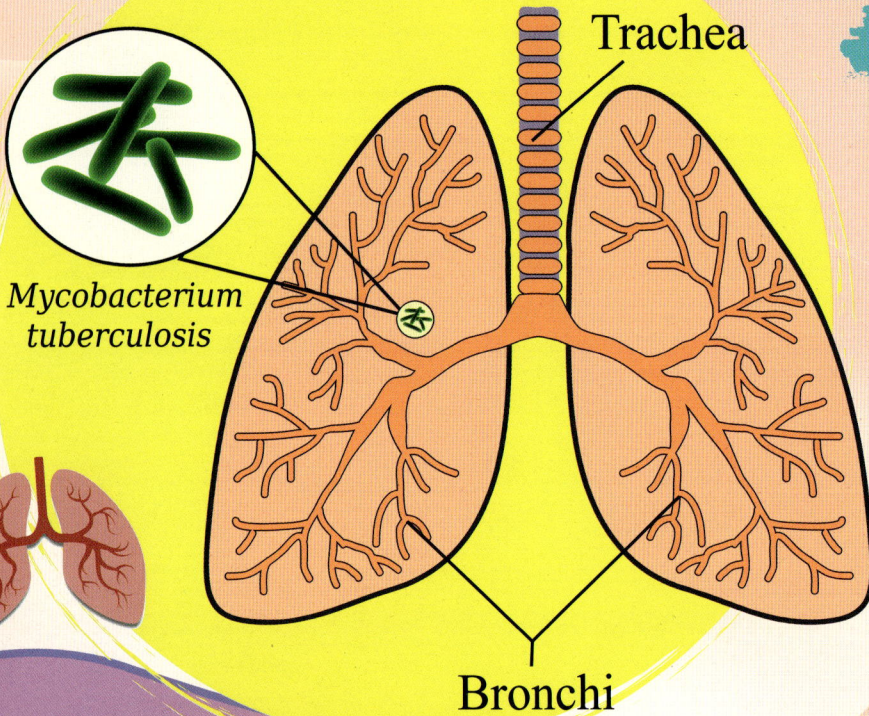

WHAT IS THE SPINAL CORD MADE UP OF?

The spinal cord is made up of a network of nerve fibres. It goes down from the brain, through a canal in the centre of the spine's bones, which protect the spinal cord. It's enveloped in cerebrospinal fluid, and meninges, which are 3 layers of membranes or tissue. The spine's nerves link the brain with nerves in most other body parts.

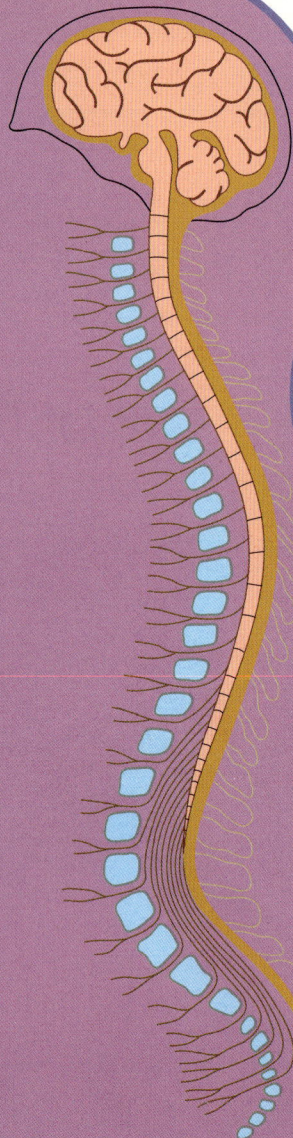

WHICH VITAMIN IS WATER—SOLUBLE?

Vitamins are called soluble if they dissolve in water. Water-soluble vitamins are not stored in the body, but carried to the tissues, and have to be consumed daily. Vitamin C and vitamins of the B family are all water-soluble. The B vitamins include biotin, folate, niacin, pantothenic acid, riboflavin, thiamine, vitamin B6, and vitamin B12.

WHERE ARE THE SALIVARY GLANDS LOCATED?

The salivary glands are located in the mouth. Whenever we bite into some food, saliva automatically occurs and the food gets mixed with it. This, in turn, makes the food to slip through the oesophagus into the stomach, and finally into the small intestine, where it gets digested.

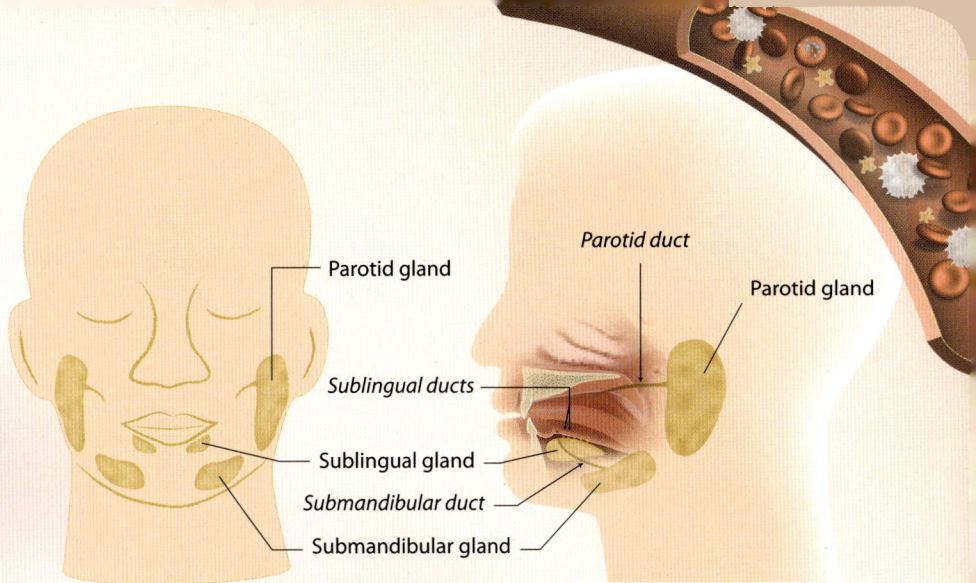

Parotid gland

Parotid duct

Parotid gland

Sublingual ducts

Sublingual gland

Submandibular duct

Submandibular gland

There are 4 main blood groups in humans and many other primates. These are A, B, AB, and O. Each of these groups can be Rh-, or Rh+. The Rh factor is a blood protein, which plays a critical role in pregnancies. Rh- is a rare blood group.

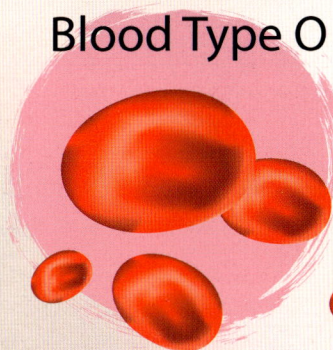

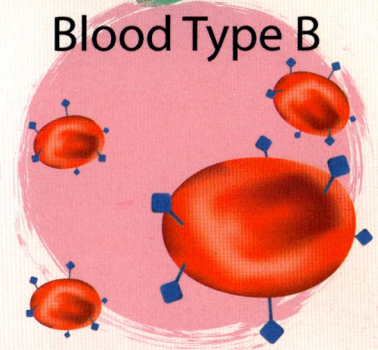

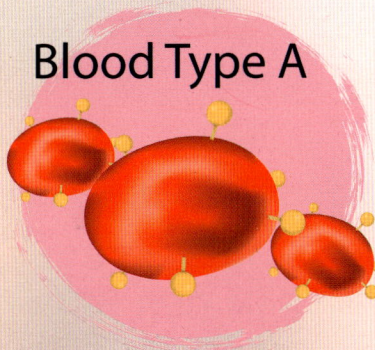

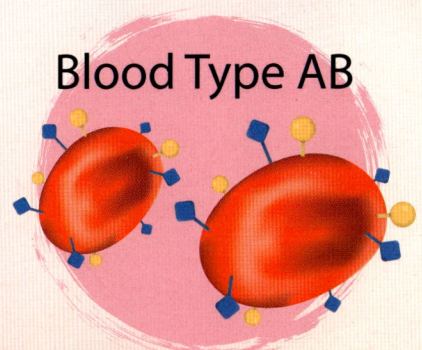

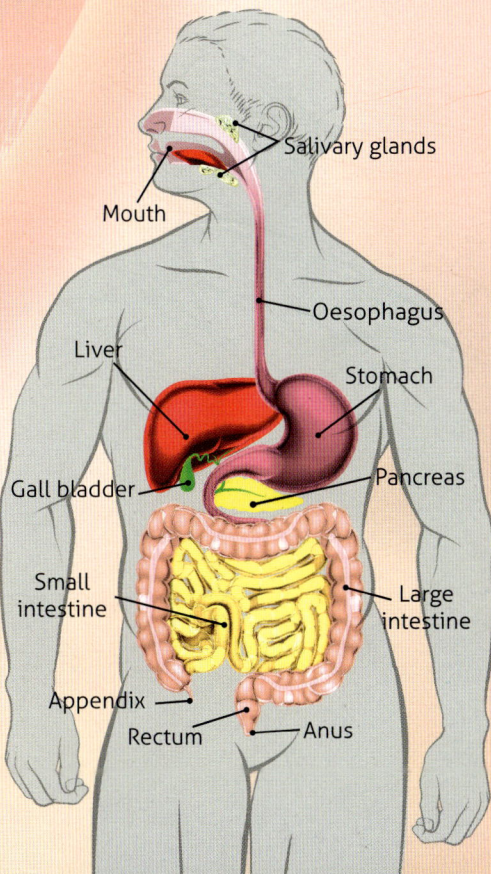

WHAT ARE THE TYPES OF BLOOD GROUPS FOUND IN HUMANS?

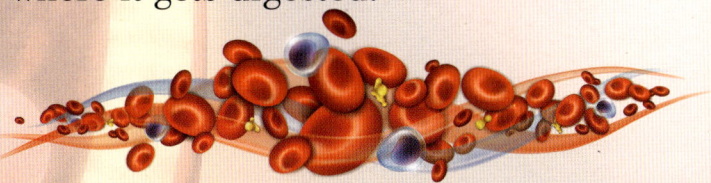

Blood Type O

Blood Type B

Blood Type A

Blood Type AB

Salivary glands

Mouth

Oesophagus

Liver

Stomach

Gall bladder

Pancreas

Small intestine

Large intestine

Appendix

Rectum

Anus

IN WHICH PART OF THE BODY DOES FOOD GET DIGESTED?

The food we eat gets digested in the small intestine. When food slips through the mouth to reach the stomach, it mixes with digestive juices and is partly digested. This thick liquid goes to the small intestine, where more enzymes complete the digestive process. The nutrients thus formed, are absorbed by tiny blood vessels of the intestinal lining.

WHAT IS THE NAME GIVEN TO DISEASES THAT OCCUR IN A SPECIFIC AREA OF THE WORLD?

Diseases that occur only in a certain part of the world, are called 'endemic'. Such diseases are always present in that particular region. Chickenpox is one such disease affecting young schoolchildren in the USA, while malaria is endemic in some parts of South Africa. Yellow fever is also endemic in tropical South America and sub-Saharan Africa.

WHICH IS THE LARGEST INTERNAL ORGAN OF OUR BODY?

The liver is the largest internal organ in the human body. It's also the heaviest organ, with an average weight of 1.6 kg in an adult human. The liver is also a gland, besides being an organ, which secretes chemicals that are used by other body parts.

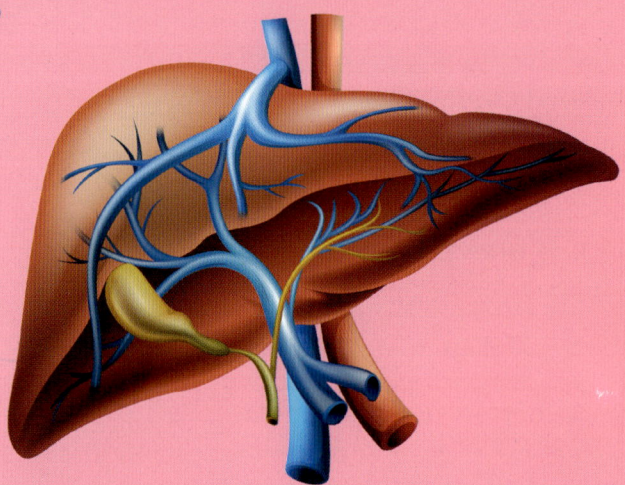

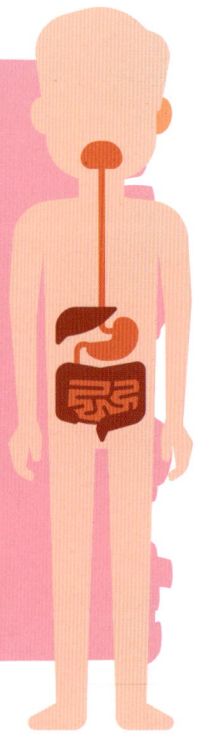

WHAT ARE THE DIFFERENT TYPES OF JOINTS IN OUR BODY?

Joints are formed when bones are linked and help these parts to work together effectively. Various types of joints are present in the body, including hinge, condyloid, ball-and-socket, pivot, plane or gliding, and saddle joints. Ball-and-socket joints are in the hips and shoulders; pivot joints are in the neck; hinge joints are in the fingers, elbows, and knees; while hands have condyloid, saddle, and plane joints.

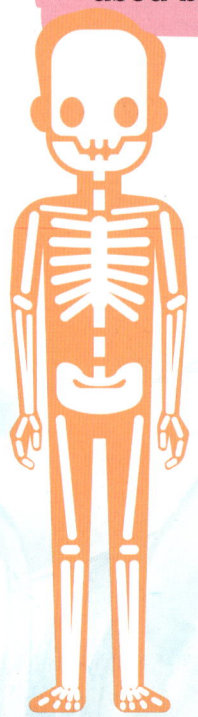

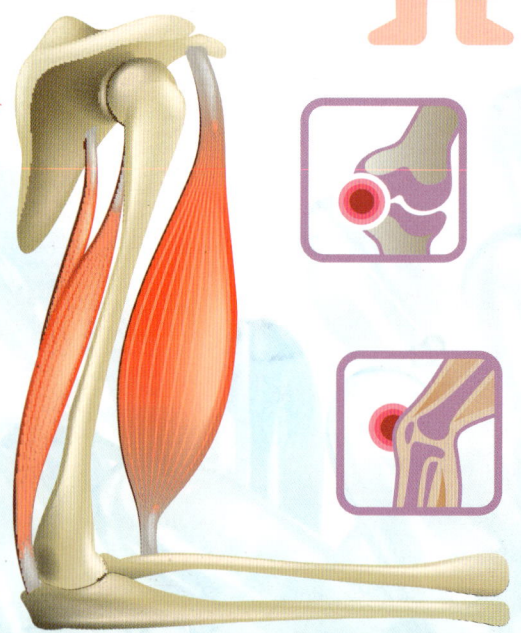

HOW MANY INTESTINES ARE THERE IN THE HUMAN BODY?

We have two types of intestines, the large and the small intestine. Food is digested in the small intestine, where it seeps into tiny cells in the intestinal lining. The water and minerals go to the large intestine. Though the large intestine is wider than the small intestine, it's only about 5ft long; whereas the narrow, small intestine that consists of coils is around 20 ft long!

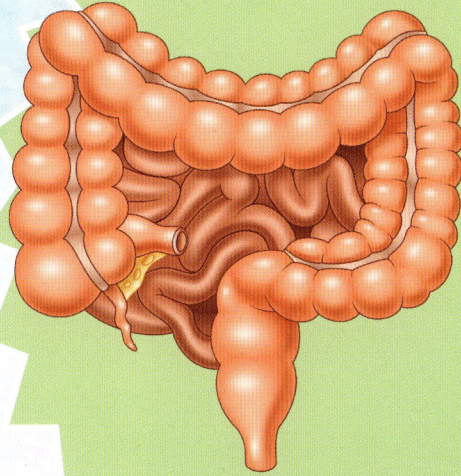

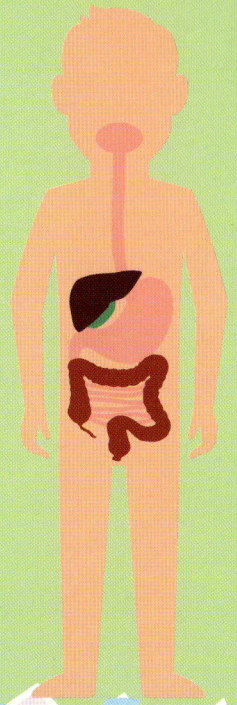

HOW IS AMMONIA CONVERTED TO UREA, AND REMOVED FROM THE BLOOD?

When amino acids are broken down, ammonia is produced, which is fatal for the body. Through carrier molecules and enzymes, the liver quickly processes ammonia and converts it into urea. Along with water urea flows out of the liver to the bloodstream. On reaching the kidneys, the blood is filtered, and the urea is sent out of the body, in the urine.

Amino acids

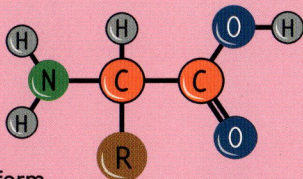

Non-ionized form of amino acids

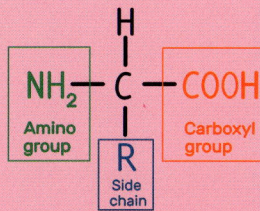

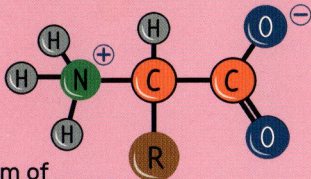

NH_2
Amino group

H
C
R
Side chain

COOH
Carboxyl group

Ionized form of amino acids (zwitterion)

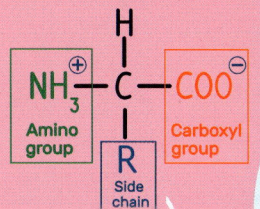

NH_3^+
Amino group

H
C
R
Side chain

COO^-
Carboxyl group

WHAT IS THE DIAPHRAGM?

The diaphragm is a dome-shaped, membranous muscle, at the bottom of the chest. It separates the thoracic cavity containing the heart and lungs, from the abdominal cavity. When we inhale, the diaphragm contracts, increasing the volume of the thoracic cavity, which allows air to be pulled into the lungs. When we exhale, the diaphragm relaxes, and the air is forced out of the lungs. It is of prime use in respiration and used when we cough, sneeze, cry, vomit, and, expel faeces or urine.

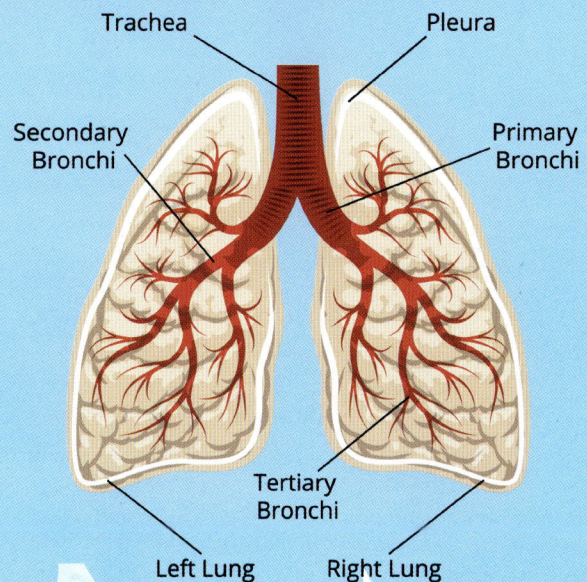

Trachea

Pleura

Secondary Bronchi

Primary Bronchi

Tertiary Bronchi

Left Lung

Right Lung

WHAT MAKES THE SENSE OF TASTE TO DIMINISH IN HUMANS?

By the time people are between 40-50 years of age, their sense of taste starts to decrease. This is because the numbers of taste buds decrease, or they start to shrink. After the age of 60, people can find it hard to distinguish sweet, sour, salty, or bitter tastes.

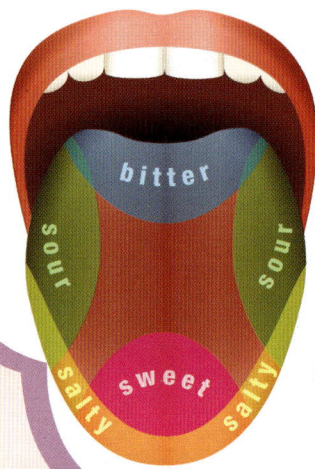

WHY ARE CARBOHYDRATES IMPORTANT?

Carbohydrates contain starch, sugar, and fibres. Sugar is a simple carb, while starch and fibre are complex carbs. Starchy foods like wheat, rice, maize or corn, barley, and oats form staple diets. Besides these, peas, potatoes, and bananas are also rich in carbohydrates, which help us when we exercise by maintaining blood glucose, and restore our muscle glucose while we rest.

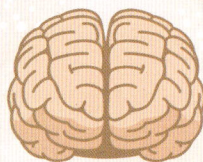

WHICH NERVES RECEIVES MESSAGES FROM THE BRAIN?

There are two main types of nerves: sensory and motor. Sensory nerves send information to the brain and spinal cord about pain, touch, heat, and cold. Motor nerves receive signals from the brain, which they transmit to the muscles, making them contract. It's the motor nerves that coordinate bodily function and movement.

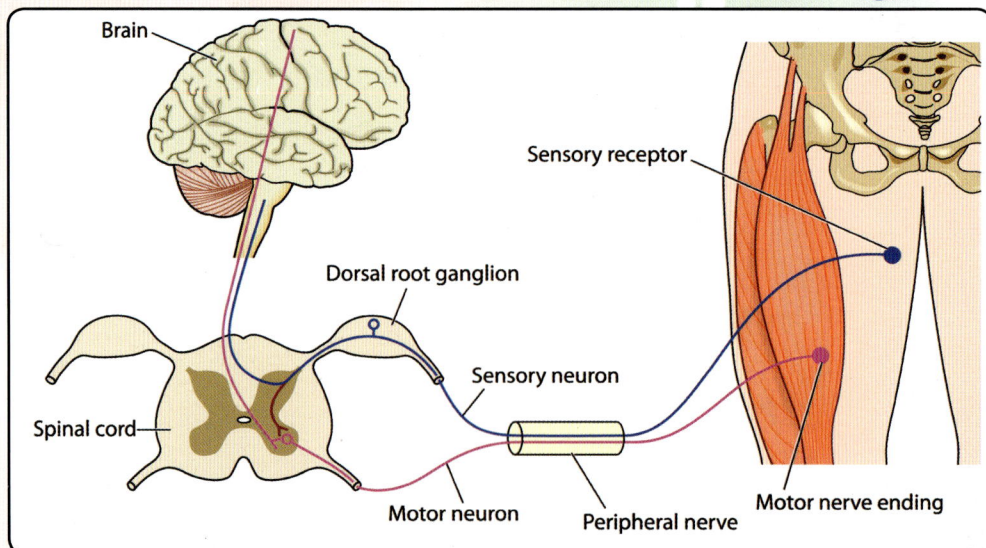

Brain

Dorsal root ganglion

Sensory receptor

Sensory neuron

Spinal cord

Motor neuron

Peripheral nerve

Motor nerve ending

WHAT CAUSES THE COMMON COLD?

The common cold is caused by many different viruses, but chiefly by the rhinovirus. An infection of the upper respiratory tract spreads by airborne droplets, which are carried when a sick person coughs or sneezes, making the cold virus enter another person's body through the mouth, nose, or eyes.

CARB, FAT AND PROTEIN

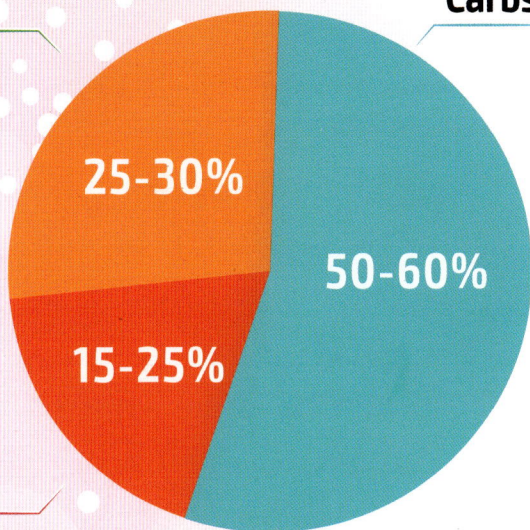

Fats

Carbs

Protein

25-30%

50-60%

15-25%

DO FATS YIELD MORE ENERGY THAN CARBOHYDRATES?

Fats contain energy, but carbohydrates process energy faster for the body. However, fats yield twice as much energy as carbohydrates! While one gram of carbohydrates gives us 4 calories, each gram of fats gives us 9 calories. Healthy unsaturated fats are found in fish, avocados, olives, cheese, nuts, seeds, and vegetable oils, particularly olive oil.

WHICH PART OF OUR BODY HELPS US TO FIGHT INFECTION?

The white blood corpuscles, or cells, of the body's immune system, help us to fight infection. Made in the bone marrow, these are present in the blood and lymph tissue and are also called lymphocytes. They constitute 1% of our blood. A drop of healthy adult blood contains between 7,000-25,000 lymphocytes, which kill germs in the body.

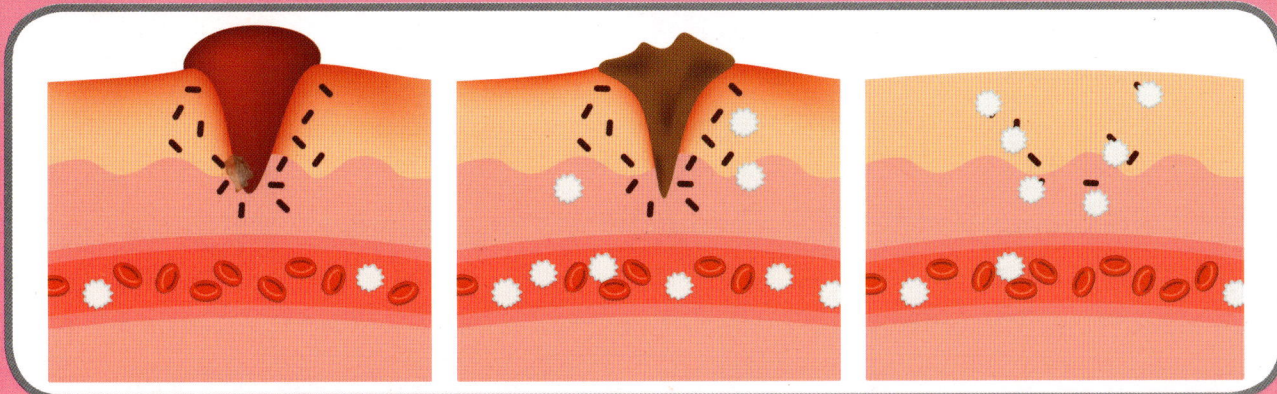

HOW MANY VALVES ARE THERE IN THE HEART?

The heart has four valves to ensure that blood flows in a single direction in the heart. The mitral and tricuspid valves regulate blood flow from the atria, to the ventricles. The aortic and pulmonary valves regulate blood flow, out of the ventricles. A leaky heart valve can impair blood flow; a serious leak can cause congestive heart failure. Open-heart surgery is mainly performed to repair or replace heart valves.

HEART VALVES

Pulmonary valve

Aortic valve

Tricuspid valve

Mitral valve

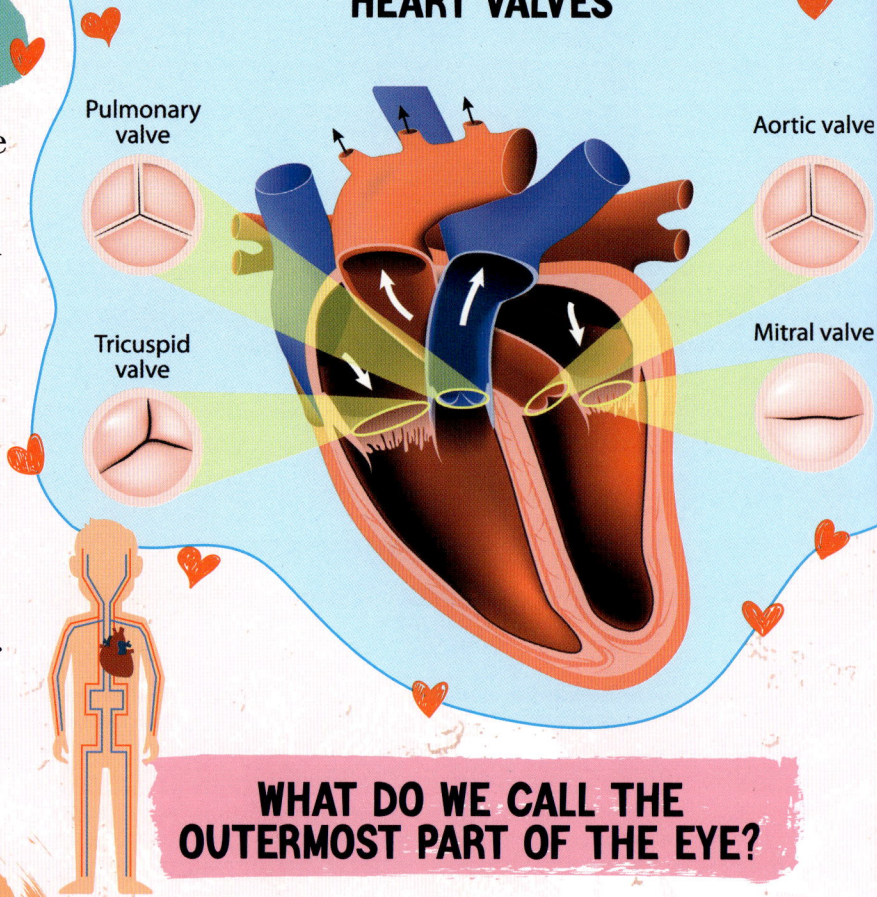

WHAT DO WE CALL THE OUTERMOST PART OF THE EYE?

The eye's outer layer contains the sclera, called the white of the eye, and the cornea, which is the clear dome at the eye's front. The sclera is tough and protects the eye, part of which is visible in front of the eye. The conjunctiva, which is a delicate, transparent membrane, covers the sclera. Light enters the eye through the cornea.

HOW SOON DOES THE BODY RECOVER BLOOD THAT IS DONATED?

Once blood is donated, the plasma in the blood is replaced in about 24 hours, but it takes around 4-6 weeks for the red cells to be restored to the normal level. The body makes 2 million new red cells in one second. There are about 10 pints of blood in an average adult's body, and less than a pint of blood is donated at one time.

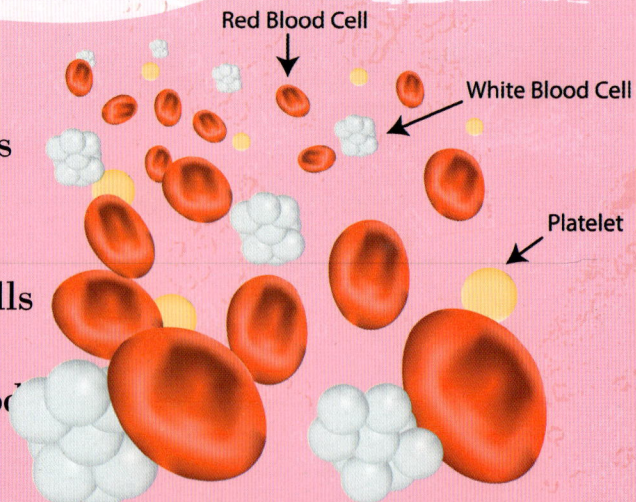

Red Blood Cell

White Blood Cell

Platelet

WHAT ARE MUSCLES, AND HOW MANY ARE THERE IN THE HUMAN BODY?

Muscles are soft tissues, which produce force and make movement possible. The body's muscular system consists of smooth, skeletal, and cardiac muscles. It's an organ system of 650 muscles, which maintains posture and helps in blood circulation. It is muscles that help humans to lift and carry things, and run, walk, push, or pull.

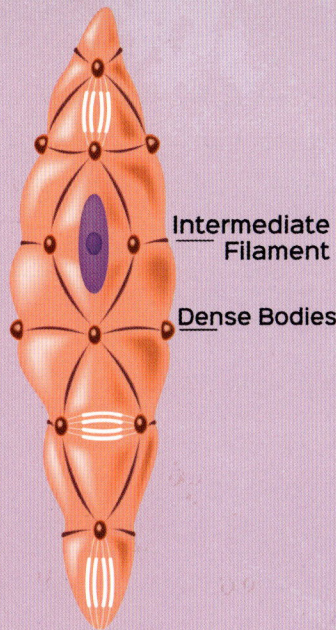

Intermediate Filament

Dense Bodies

Nucleus

Thin Filament

Thick Filament

Relaxed

Contracted

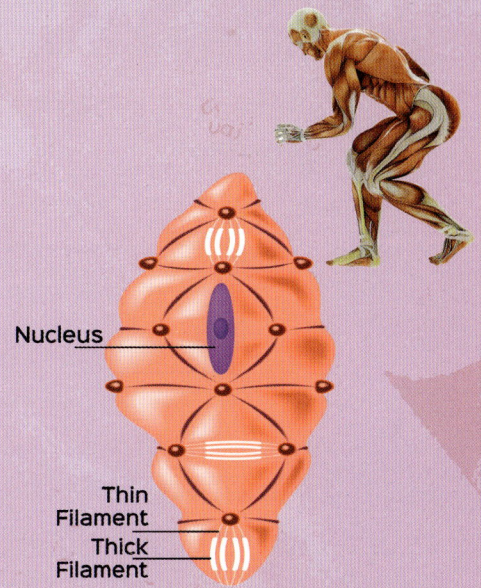

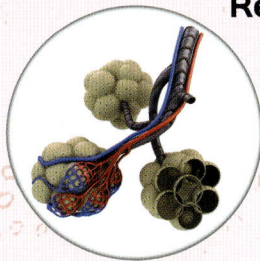

WHAT IS THE AMOUNT OF OXYGEN THAT WE INHALE FROM THE AIR?

The air that we breathe contains around 21% oxygen. But air also contains 78% nitrogen, and small amounts of other gases including carbon dioxide (CO_2), argon, and methane. While we inhale about 20%-21% oxygen, we exhale around 15% of it, consuming nearly 5% oxygen in each breath, which is changed into CO_2.

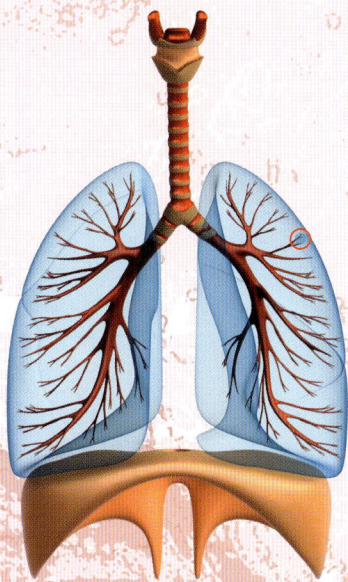

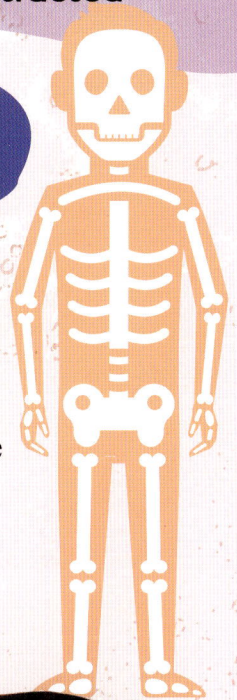

WHAT IS THE FUNCTION OF THE KIDNEYS?

Located in the upper abdominal cavity, our two bean-shaped kidneys rest against the back muscles, opposite each other. The most important function they perform is the renal function. Besides excretion of waste matter, the kidneys maintain water fluid balance in the body, and, regulate blood pressure and production of red blood cells.

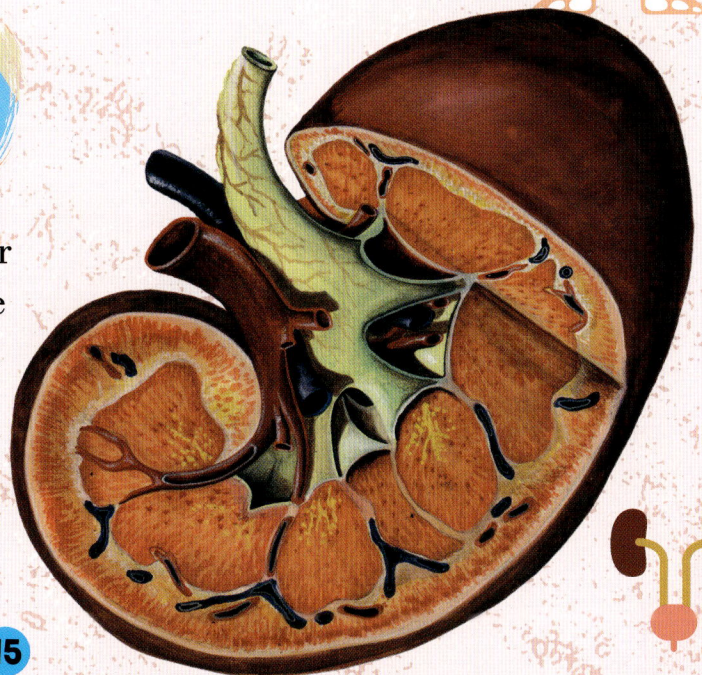

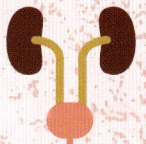

WHAT IS HYPOTHERMIA?

Hypothermia means having a low body temperature, below 95°F. This is due to exposure to extremely cold weather, such as swimming in very cold waters, or a snowstorm. Mild hypothermia causes people to shiver and have mental confusion but can be easily treated. Moderate hypothermia becomes harder to treat; while severe hypothermia can be fatal, and people need immediate medical attention.

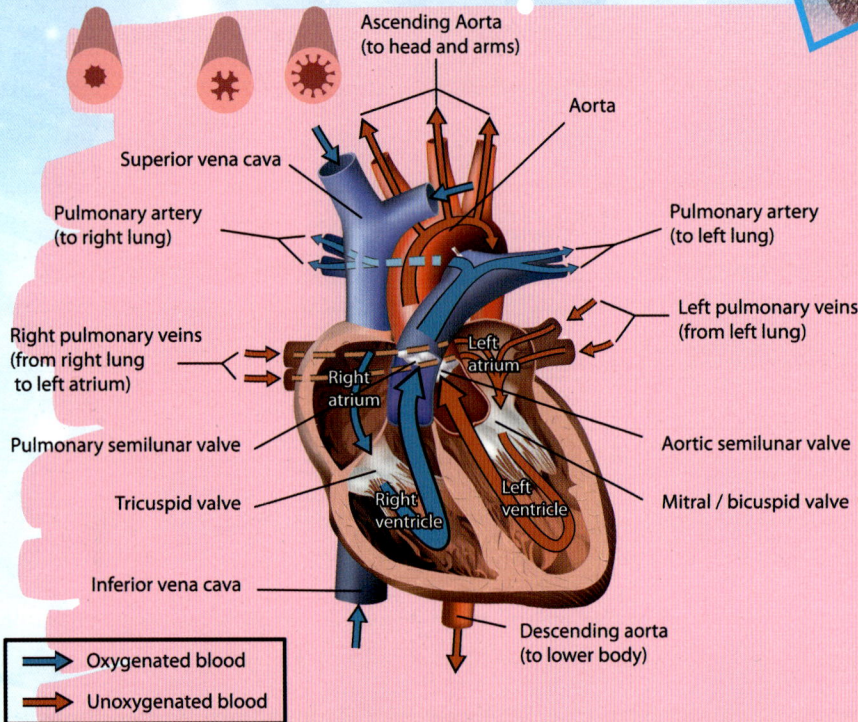

Ascending Aorta (to head and arms)

Aorta

Superior vena cava

Pulmonary artery (to right lung)

Pulmonary artery (to left lung)

Right pulmonary veins (from right lung to left atrium)

Left pulmonary veins (from left lung)

Left atrium

Right atrium

Pulmonary semilunar valve

Aortic semilunar valve

Tricuspid valve

Mitral / bicuspid valve

Right ventricle

Left ventricle

Inferior vena cava

Descending aorta (to lower body)

→ Oxygenated blood
→ Unoxygenated blood

HOW DOES BLOOD ENTER OUR INTERNAL ORGANS?

The heart is a key part of the body's circulatory system. The network of blood vessels in the heart, including veins, arteries, and capillaries, transport blood to and from all body parts. When blood enters the heart's left atrium, it's pumped into the left ventricle. Oxygen-rich blood from here is sent to the rest of the body, through the aorta.

CAN SCURVY BE CURED?

In the past, sailors particularly suffered from scurvy. Dr James Lind, a Scotsman, discovered by chance that it could be prevented by the intake of citrus fruits! A lack of vitamin C first makes the affected person feel weak, tired, and with sore arms and legs. If untreated, it can cause gum disease, falling of teeth, hair loss or brittle hair, and decreased red cells. Scurvy is easily treated by increasing the intake of vitamin C.

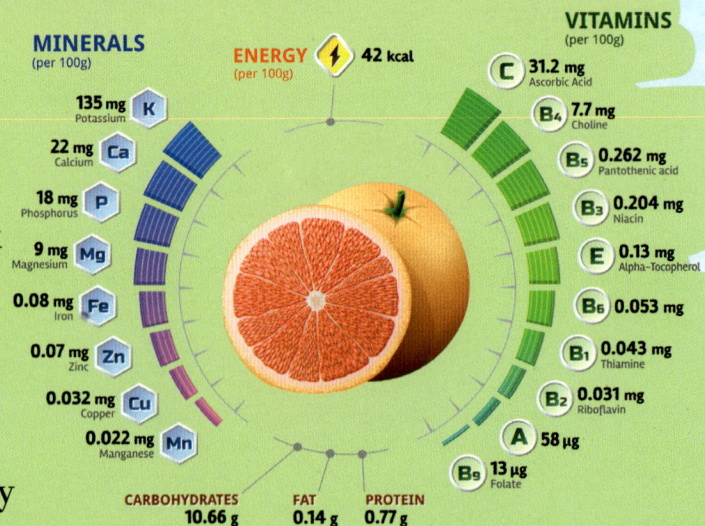

MINERALS (per 100g)

ENERGY (per 100g) ⚡ 42 kcal

VITAMINS (per 100g)

135 mg K Potassium

22 mg Ca Calcium

18 mg P Phosphorus

9 mg Mg Magnesium

0.08 mg Fe Iron

0.07 mg Zn Zinc

0.032 mg Cu Copper

0.022 mg Mn Manganese

C 31.2 mg Ascorbic Acid

B₄ 7.7 mg Choline

B₅ 0.262 mg Pantothenic acid

B₃ 0.204 mg Niacin

E 0.13 mg Alpha-Tocopherol

B₆ 0.053 mg

B₁ 0.043 mg Thiamine

B₂ 0.031 mg Riboflavin

A 58 µg

B₉ 13 µg Folate

CARBOHYDRATES 10.66 g

FAT 0.14 g

PROTEIN 0.77 g

WHAT ARE THE SOUNDS THAT WE CAN NORMALLY HEAR?

The sounds that we normally hear, have frequencies or pitch ranging from 20 to 20,000 hertz (Hz). The important sounds we usually hear daily fall within the range of 250-6,000 Hz. The loudness or intensity of sounds we hear is measured in decibels (dB). We can hear sounds as low as 0 dB! But sounds above 85 dB can cause hearing loss.

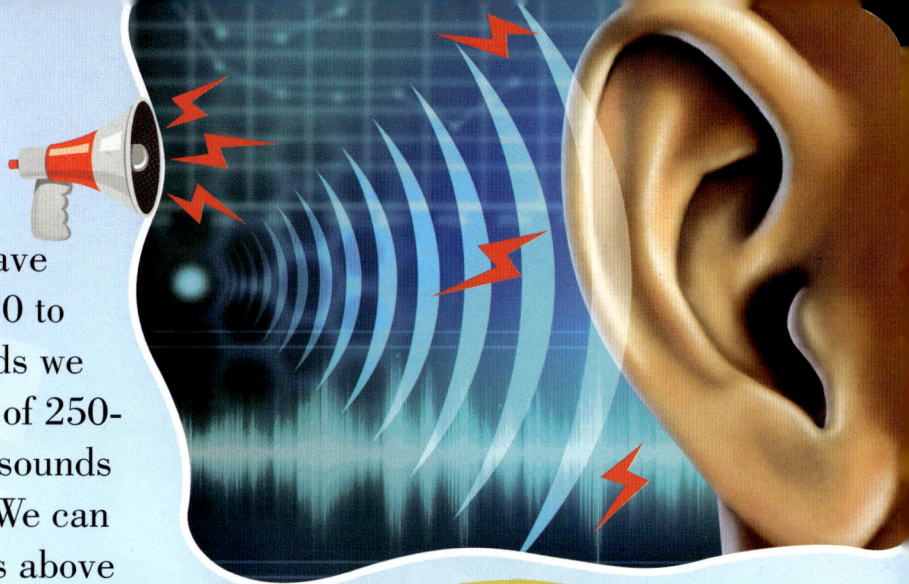

HOW MANY BONES ARE THERE IN THE HUMAN EAR, AND WHAT IS THE ROLE OF THE PINNA?

The ear bones, or Auditory Ossicles, are 3 tiny bones in the centre of the human ear, called: the malleus, or hammer; the incus, or anvil; and, the stapes, or stirrup. The only visible part of the ear is the ear flap, called the pinna. Sound travels through the pinna to the external auditory canal that ends at the eardrum, causing the eardrum and ossicles to vibrate, and reaches the cochlea in the inner ear, which converts sound into nerve impulses that are sent to the brain.

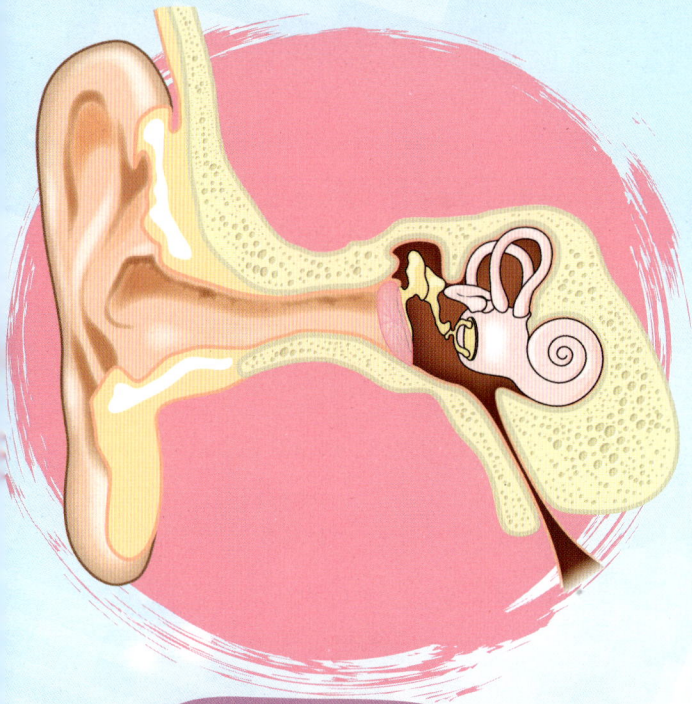

WHAT CAUSES THALASSAEMIA?

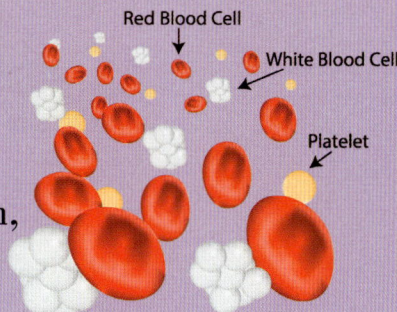

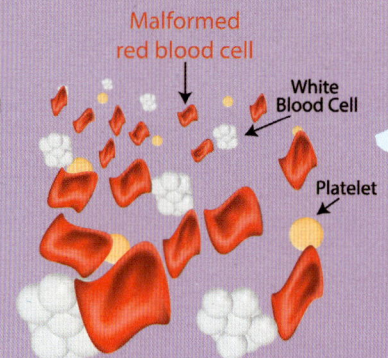

Thalassaemia is caused by a genetic disorder. Those who suffer from thalassaemia, produce little or no haemoglobin, which helps red blood cells to transport oxygen in the body. Due to this, patients fall short of breath, tire very fast, and need repeated blood transfusions. It can be managed with treatment, but till now there is no cure for thalassaemia.

NORMAL

Red Blood Cell

White Blood Cell

Platelet

THALASSAEMIA

Malformed red blood cell

White Blood Cell

Platelet

WHAT IS RESPIRATION?

Respiration is the most crucial part of our lives, and our lungs help us to breathe in oxygen and breathe out carbon dioxide. We can stay without food or water for some time, but not oxygen. The respiratory system comprises nasal air passages, throat, windpipe, and two tube-like bronchi, which carry air to the lungs. Through the lungs, oxygen enters the bloodstream, while the waste air or carbon dioxide is breathed out.

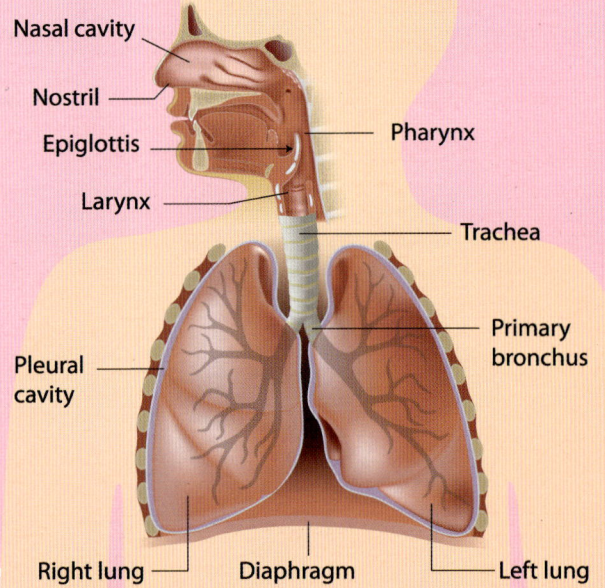

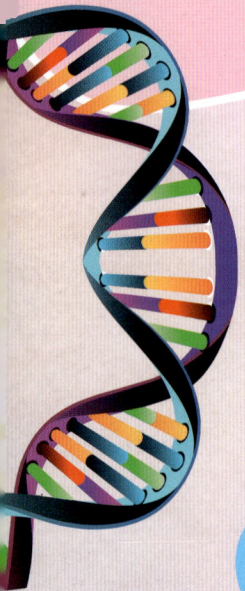

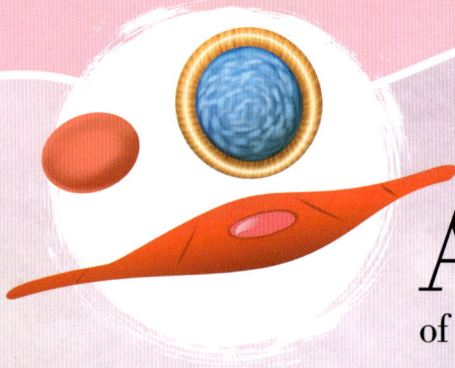

Nasal cavity

Nostril

Epiglottis

Larynx

Pharynx

Trachea

Primary bronchus

Pleural cavity

Right lung

Diaphragm

Left lung

HOW MANY TYPES OF CELLS ARE THERE IN OUR BODY?

All humans, animals, and plants are made up of cells. Humans have around 200 types of cells, and within these, 20 different types of structures exist. Different cells perform different tasks. The major cell types co-ordinating functions all through the body are the muscle, nerve, and red blood cells.

RICKETS

WHICH ARE THE DISEASES THAT CAN AFFECT OUR BONES?

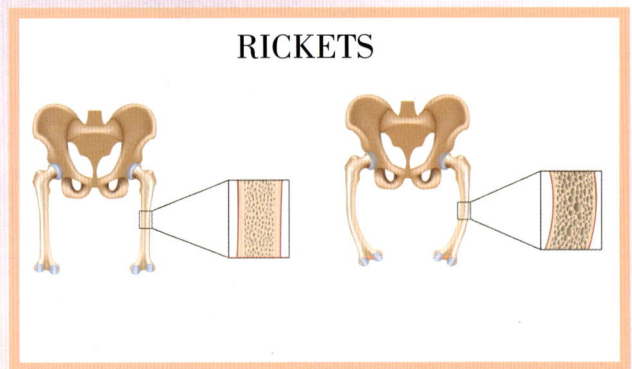

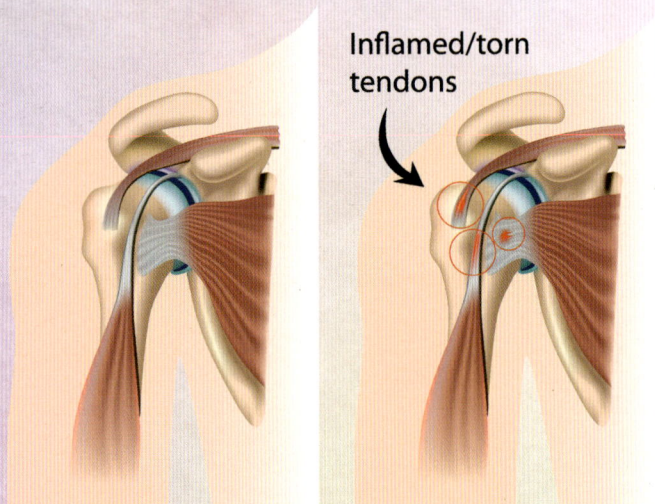

Inflamed/torn tendons

Injury to bones, as well as disease, can be a major cause of abnormality of the human skeletal system. There are various bone diseases, including osteoarthritis, rickets, osteosarcoma or bone cancer, osteomalacia, osteochondroma, osteoma, Paget disease of bone, marble bone disease, and cleidocranial dysostosis.

SHOULDER INJURY

HOW MANY PAIRS OF RIBS DO WE HAVE?

Humans have 12 pairs of ribs, placed on or between the thoracic vertebrae in the rib cage, which protects the organs that it surrounds. The first 7 pairs are attached by costal cartilages directly to the sternum, and are called 'true ribs'. The 8th-10th rib pairs do not join the sternum, and are called 'false ribs'. The last 2 pairs are not attached to the sternum or to another rib, and are thus known as 'floating ribs'.

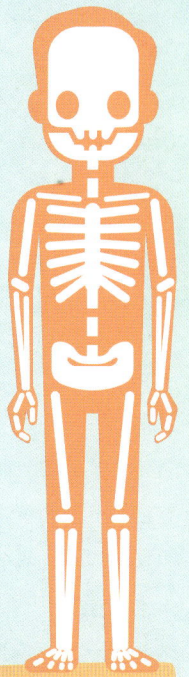

HOW MANY DIFFERENT ODOURS CAN THE HUMAN NOSE DISTINGUISH?

It was earlier believed that our nose could differentiate between 10,000 different odours. Presently, US scientists have ascertained that our nose can detect around 1 trillion different odours! As we inhale, the odour molecules in the air, bind to receptors within our nose and send signals to the brain.

WHAT CAUSES EPILEPSY AND HOW IS IT TREATED?

Epilepsy is marked by seizures, caused by faulty electrical activity in the brain. It's a common neurological disorder, affecting people of any age. Among other things, the affected person may have convulsions with arms or legs jerking; short spells of fainting fit; or, suddenly become stiff. Most forms of epilepsy are incurable but can be managed with medication, a special diet, or surgery.

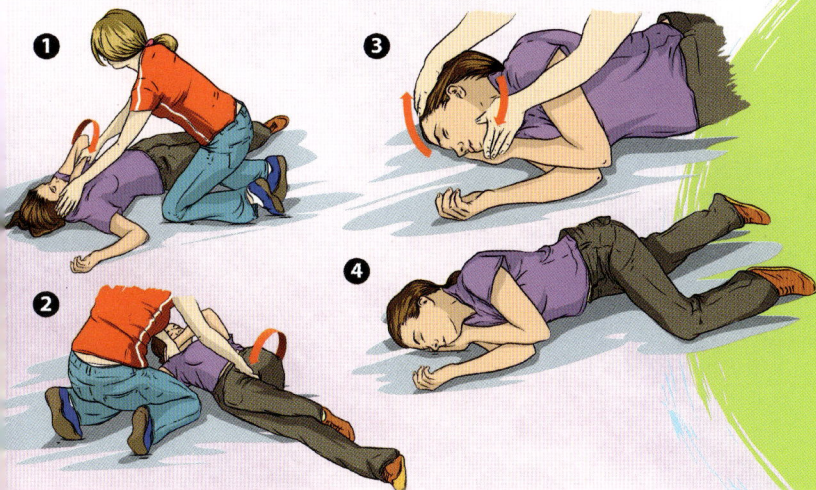

WHAT IS THE RATE OF THE HUMAN HEARTBEAT?

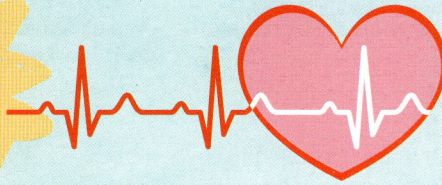

The human heart beats at the rate of 72 beats in a minute, around 100,000 times in a day! The heart rate is an important indicator of health and measures the number of times that the heart beats, or contracts and relaxes, within a minute. The heart rate increases during activity, but averages between 60-100 beats when a person is resting.

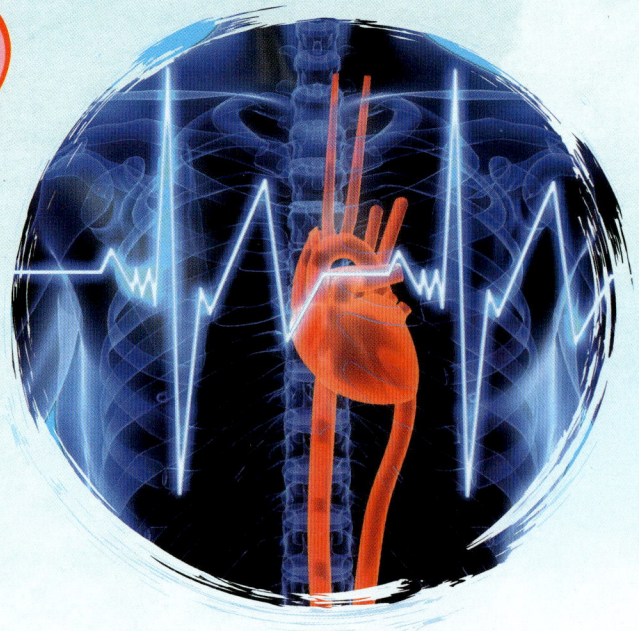

CAN CERTAIN FOODS REDUCE EPILEPTIC SEIZURES?

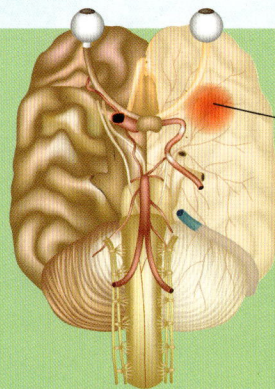

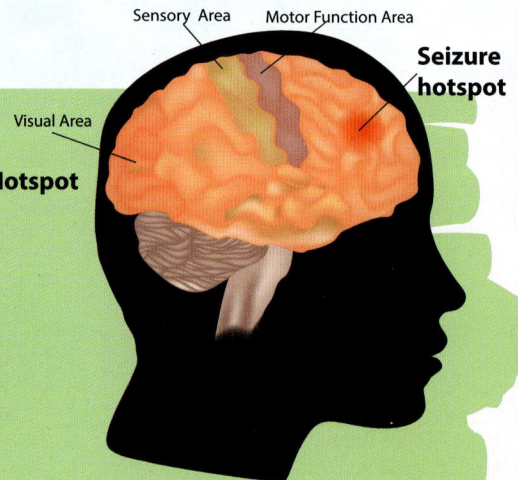

Sensory Area

Motor Function Area

Seizure hotspot

Visual Area

Hotspot

Around 60% of people epileptics become seizure-free after medication. A special low-carb, high-fat diet, is also recommended, including bacon, butter, eggs, mayonnaise, heavy cream, nuts, fish, cheeses, vegetables, and fruits, especially avocados. Studies have found that 29% of patients taking the modified Atkins diet and 32% of patients taking a ketogenic diet, gained by 50% or more reduction in seizures, after the diet!

HOW DO OUR TEETH HELP US TO EAT OUR FOOD?

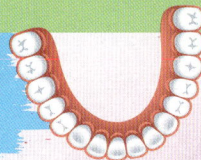

Teeth help us to chew our food properly so that it is easily digested. Adult humans have 32 teeth, made up of incisors, canines, and molars. We cut and shear our food using the 8 sharp, incisor teeth at the front. The canines or long, pointed teeth, on either side of the incisors, are also used to bite food. The molars or large, flat teeth at the back of the mouth, help to grind food during chewing.

WHAT ARE THE CONDITIONS THAT HYDROTHERAPY CAN CURE?

Hydrotherapy is a form of alternative medicine, using water for relaxation and to treat certain diseases. The water may be used internally or externally, at varying temperatures, and includes warm water baths, steam baths, compresses, wraps, and pool exercises. It has benefitted those suffering from knee osteoarthritis and rheumatoid arthritis to an extent and used in recovery after team sports.

WHAT IS THE NORMAL BLOOD PRESSURE OF A HUMAN ADULT?

The normal blood pressure of an adult human being is 120/80. When people fall sick or get a shock, their blood pressure is likely to fluctuate. It can increase or drop down drastically, causing weakness and exhaustion. Hypertension is when people have high blood pressure; while if the blood pressure is low, it's called hypotension.

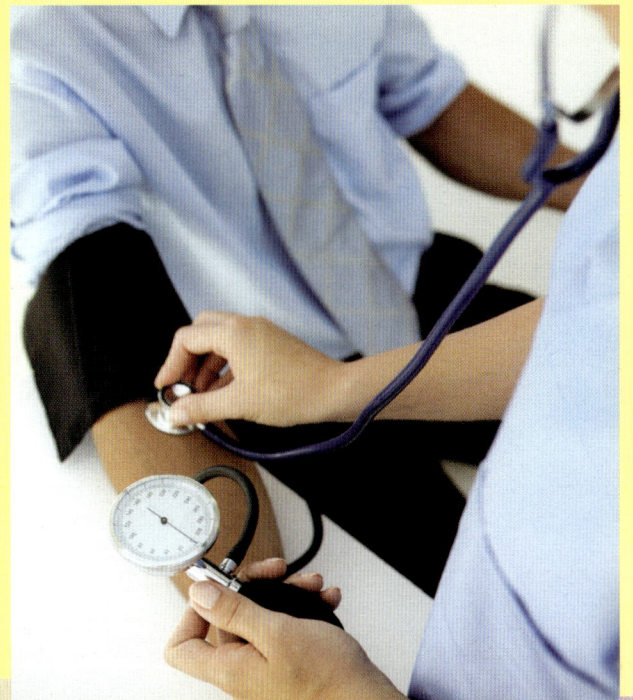

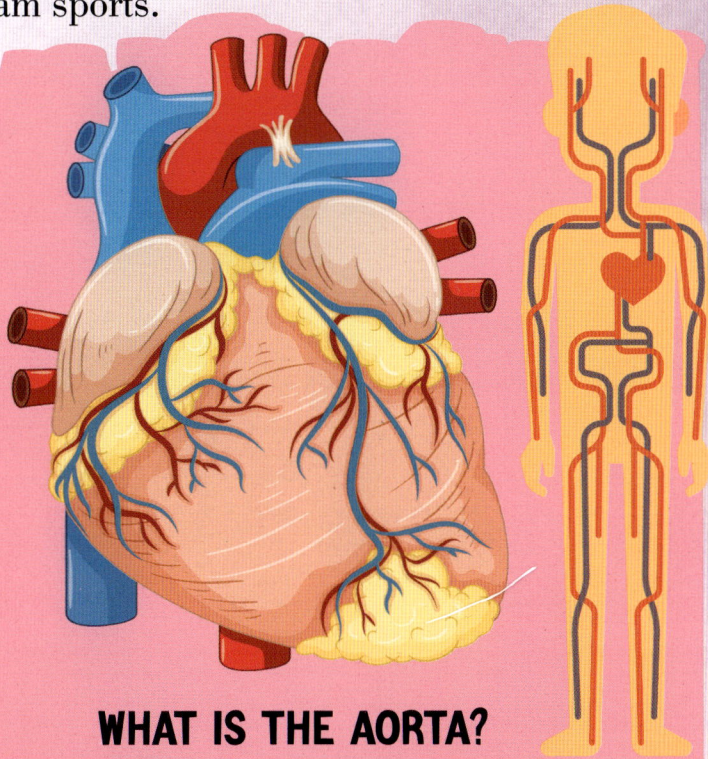

WHAT IS THE AORTA?

The aorta is the main and largest artery in the heart. It starts at the top of the heart's left ventricle, which is the muscular pumping chamber for the heart. Blood is pumped from the left ventricle, through the aortic valve into the aorta, which sends it to the rest of the body. At times, the effects of high blood pressure, smoking, or certain disorders can cause the aorta to become enlarged, which can be fatal if untreated.

Factual

Imagination

It is the right part of the body that is controlled by the left brain, and vice versa! So, the brain's left side controls the right part of the body's movement, vision, hearing, and sensation. While the brain's right side has similar control over the left part of the body.

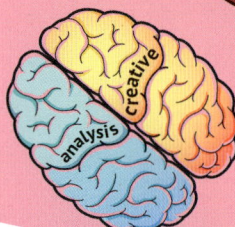

analysis creative

AMONGST HUMANS, WHO SMELLS THE MOST?

Amongst men, women, children, and babies, it is babies that smell the most. It is because they are helpless and unable to look after themselves. Until someone attends to them, they can be lying in wet clothes, or spoil their clothes as they bring out milk very often.

WHY DO WE CALL SOME PEOPLE 'LEFT–HANDED'?

Some people use their left hand to write, eat, drive, or play, like most of us use our right hand. This is because, in these people, it is the right part of the brain that controls their body movements.

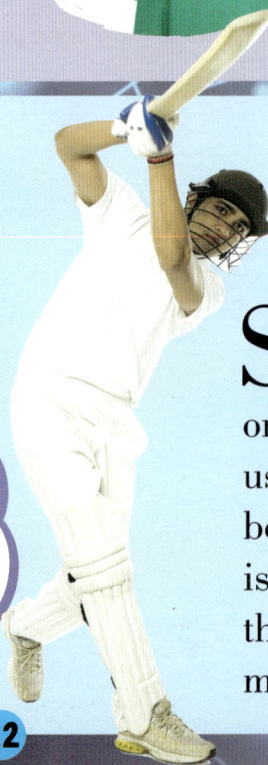

HOW MANY CHROMOSOMES ARE THERE IN EACH OF OUR BODY CELLS?

Humans have 23 pairs of chromosomes in each cell. 22 pairs of these string-shaped structures are identical in females and males and called autosomes. In the 23rd pair, females have two 'X' chromosomes and males have an 'X' and a 'Y' chromosome, which decide the sex of a baby. Chromosomes mainly comprise the DNA, carrying hereditary material, which decides the colour of the eyes, hair, etc. in a child.

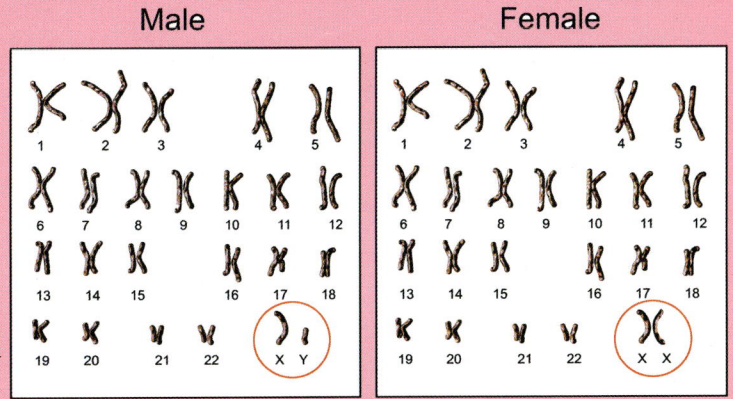

Male

Female

WHAT IS THE FUNCTION OF TENDONS?

Tendons are tough bands of fibrous, connective tissue. Also called a sinew, a tendon is similar to a ligament, as both are made up of collagen. Tendons link muscles to bones and can withstand tension, but an injury can cause pain, stiffness, and weakness in the affected area. A tendon is capable of self-repair usually and heals after rest.

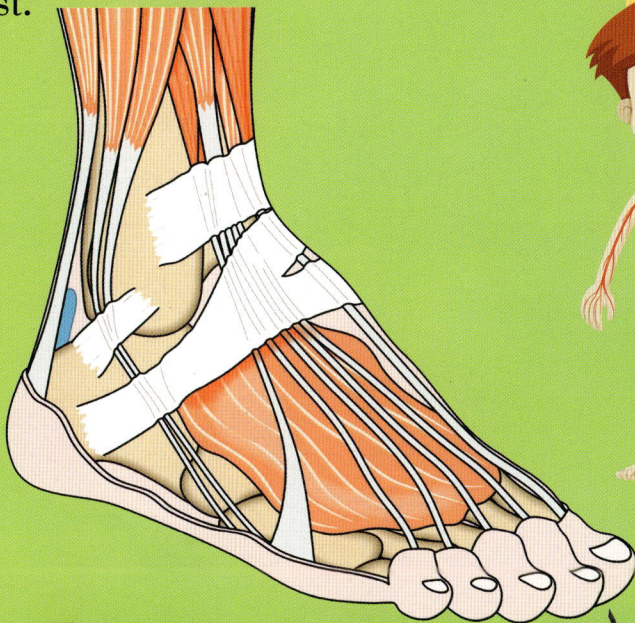

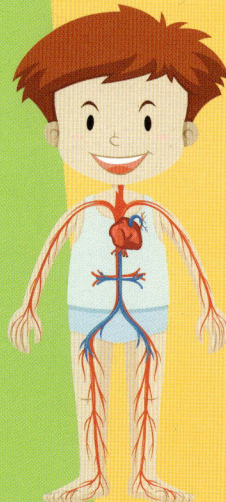

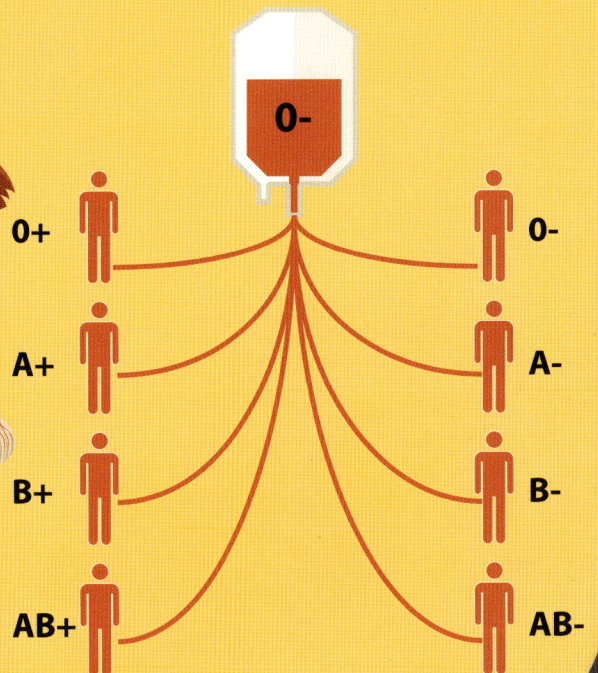

WHICH IS THE UNIVERSAL BLOOD GROUP?

The universal blood group is O negative [O-]. People having O- type blood are called 'universal donors', as their blood can be given to anyone if the need arises. Those with AB+ blood are called 'universal recipients'. On any other blood type, the proteins or antigens on the surface of the red blood cells can harm the recipient's immune system.

O-

O+   O-
A+   A-
B+   B-
AB+   AB-

O- NEGATIVE
BLOOD GROUP

23

WHY ARE SOME BABIES CALLED PREMATURE?

Sometimes, when a baby is born before its due time, which means before the mother has completed 9 months of pregnancy, then it is called a premature baby. Such babies are often weak, and particularly if a baby is born in the 7th month, it has to be kept in an incubator, under observation, till doctors are sure it will remain fine out of the incubator.

WHAT DO ULTRASOUNDS AND X—RAYS DO?

With the advancement of scientific technology, it's now possible to take pictures of organs inside our bodies and study them for signs of illness. X-rays, ultrasounds, and magnetic resonance imaging (MRIs) do exactly that, though different methods are used in each process by a skilled technician, to help doctors find the problem or rule out a doubt.

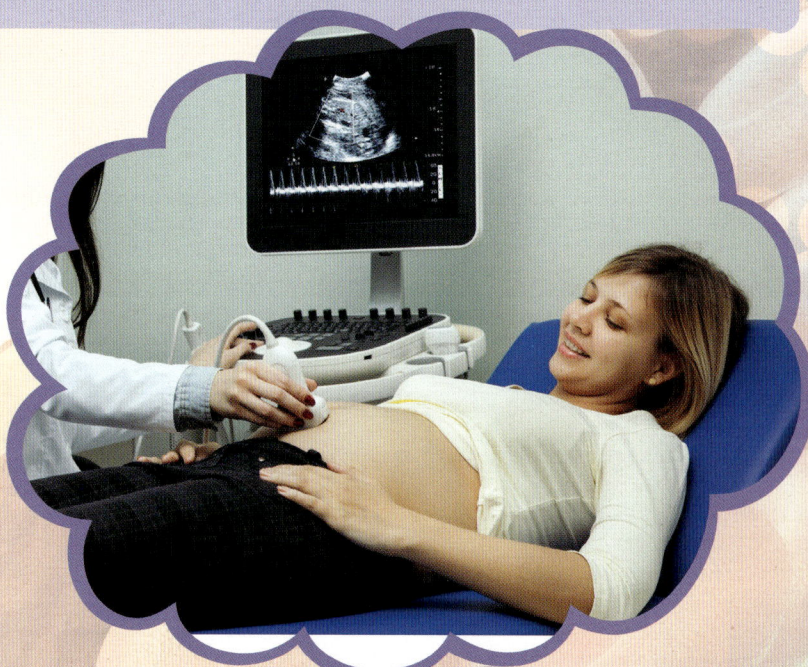

HOW MUCH OF THE BODY'S WEIGHT IS MADE UP OF BONES?

About 14% of the body's weight is made up of bones, which form the framework of the human body. Though our bones are strong, yet they are one-half water! Most of our bones have a hard layer of compact bone with a cavity in the middle, full of jelly-like bone marrow. The largest bone is the thighbone, while the smallest one is in the ears.

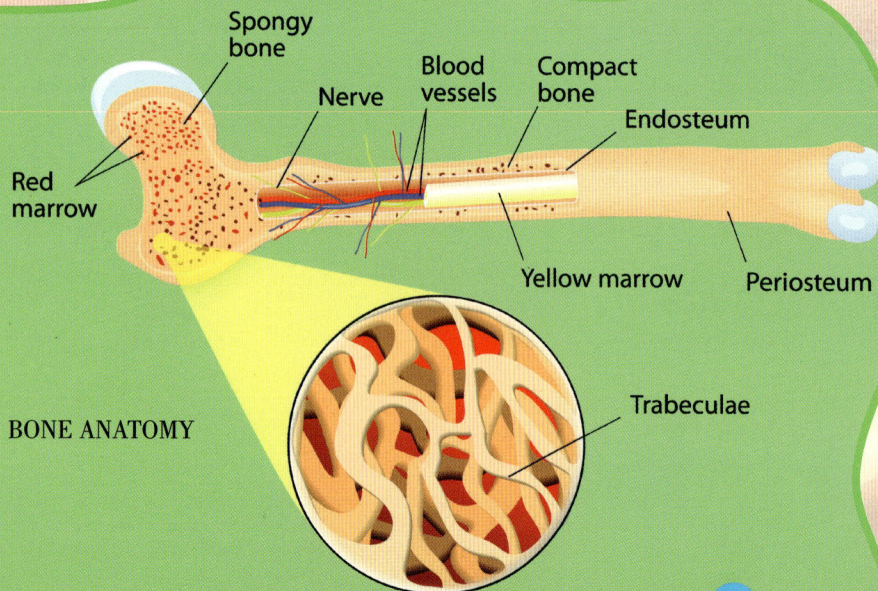

Spongy bone
Nerve
Blood vessels
Compact bone
Endosteum
Red marrow
Yellow marrow
Periosteum
Trabeculae

BONE ANATOMY

AMONGST HUMANS, PLANTS, AND ANIMALS, WHO MAKE THEIR OWN VITAMINS?

Plants make their own vitamins and food, through the process we call photosynthesis, during the day. Chlorophyll, a plant pigment, captures energy from sunlight, which converts water and carbon dioxide into oxygen and sugars. The carbon dioxide is absorbed by plants, while they release oxygen, contrary to what humans and animals do.

WHICH VITAMIN IS MADE IN OUR BODY?

The action of the sun on our skin results in the creation of Vitamin D! This 'sunshine vitamin' keeps our bones healthy, gives strength to our muscles, and makes our immune system strong. And it's possible by merely exposing the skin to the sun's ultraviolet B rays. Besides, foods such as egg yolks, cheese, fatty fish, some brands of yogurt, soy milk, orange juice, and cereals are good supplements of this vitamin.

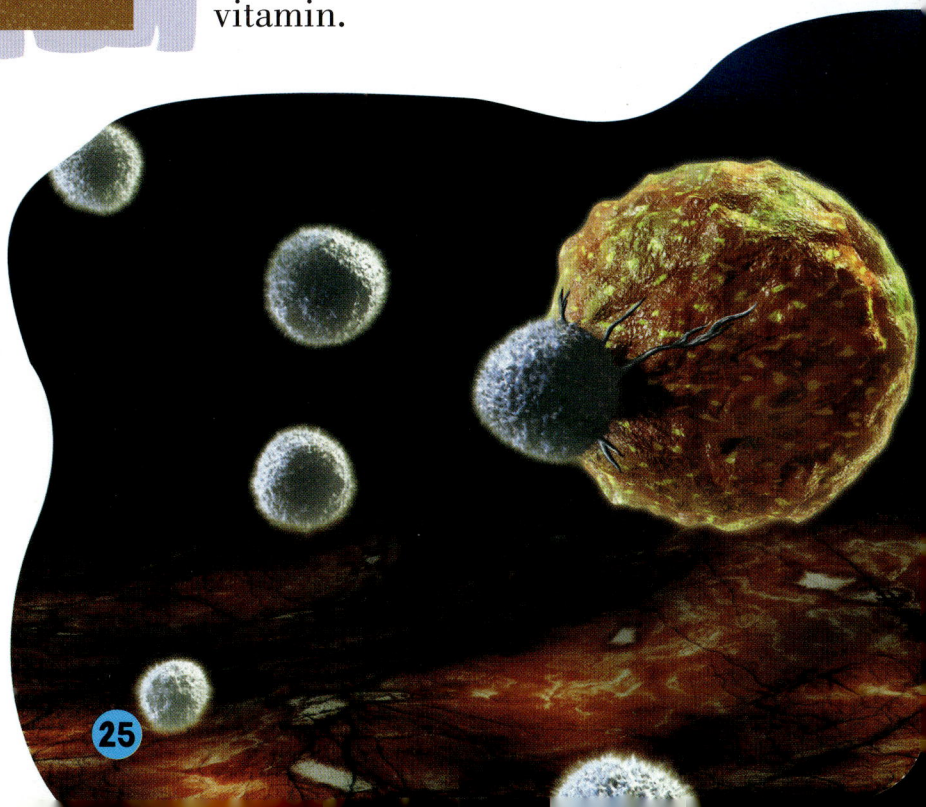

HOW DO MALIGNANT CELLS BEHAVE IN CANCER?

When the body's immune system breaks down, the white blood cells that are meant to help the body, start destroying other cells. This results in people falling prey to fatal diseases, such as cancer. In such illnesses, the malignant cells keep multiplying.

WHICH LAYER OF TISSUE IS FORMED BY BLOOD IN OUR BODY?

The 4 chief tissue layers in the body are epithelial, connective, muscle, and nervous. The connective tissue is found in between different tissue layers and organs. It protects organs, binds skin with muscle, and muscle with bones. One form of the supporting connective tissue is the fluid or liquid connective tissue, which is formed by blood or lymph.

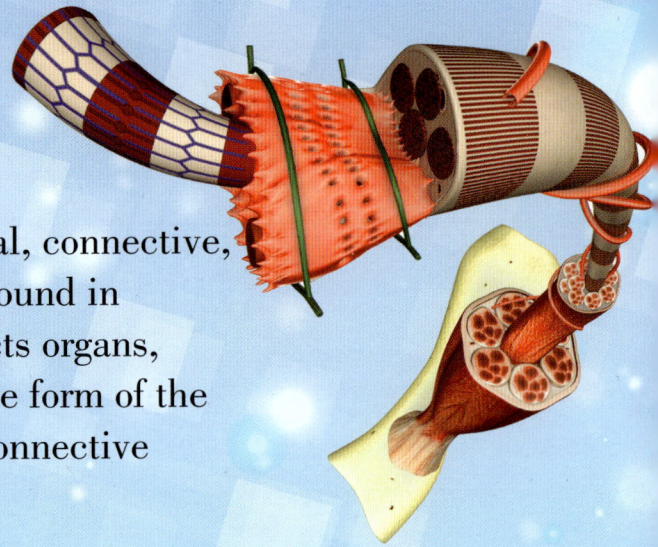

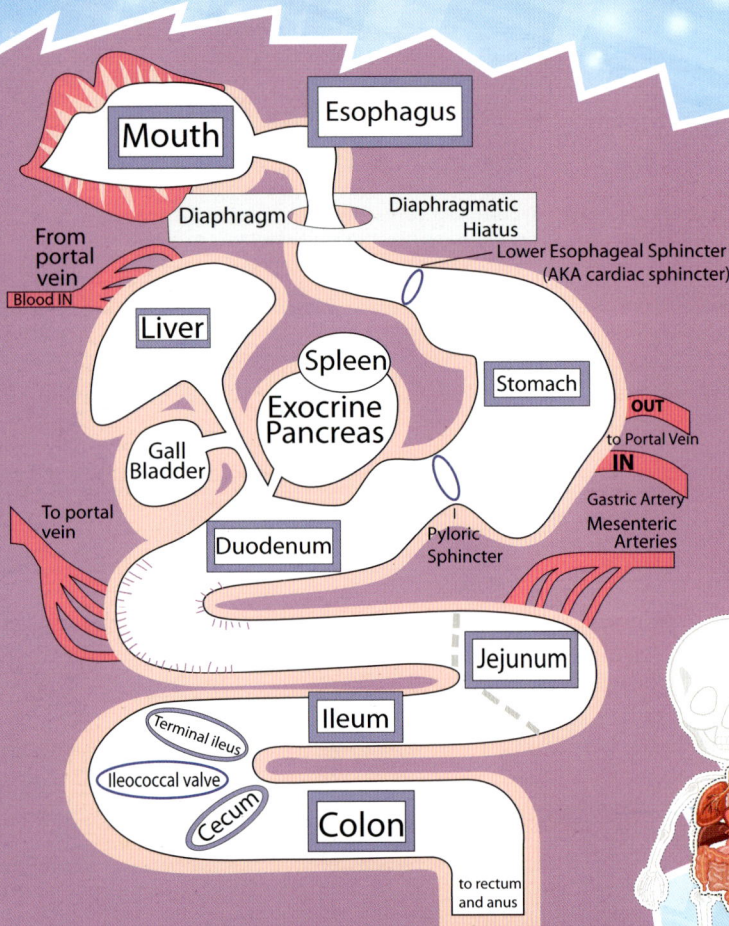

Mouth
Esophagus
Diaphragm
Diaphragmatic Hiatus
From portal vein
Blood IN
Lower Esophageal Sphincter (AKA cardiac sphincter)
Liver
Spleen
Stomach
Exocrine Pancreas
OUT
to Portal Vein
IN
Gall Bladder
Gastric Artery
Mesenteric Arteries
To portal vein
Duodenum
Pyloric Sphincter
Jejunum
Ileum
Terminal ileus
Ileococcal valve
Cecum
Colon
to rectum and anus

WHICH ENZYMES HELP TO BREAK DOWN FOOD?

Digestive enzymes break down food in the stomach, from where food flows as a partly-digested liquid to the small intestine, for digestion to be completed. The 3 main sorts of digestive enzymes are protease, lipase, and amylase. Proteases split proteins into tiny peptides and amino acids. Lipases break down lipids, or fats and oils, into fatty acids and glycerol. Amylases convert carbs such as starch, into sugar.

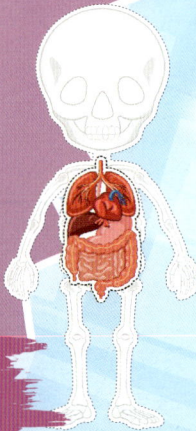

WHY DO STONES FORM IN THE GALLBLADDER OR KIDNEY?

GALLBLADDER STONE

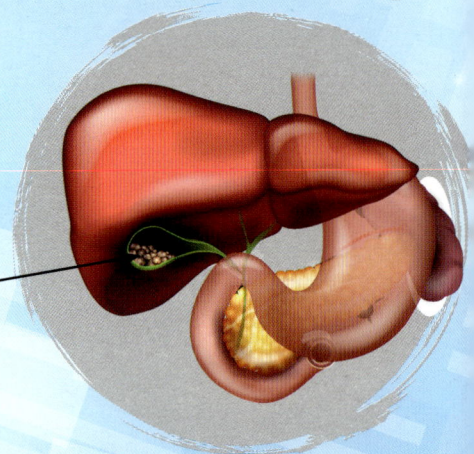

The gallbladder holds bile, a digestive fluid, which is released in the small intestine. When the bile has a high amount of bilirubin or cholesterol, it forms stones in the gallbladder. Similarly, in the kidneys, when there are too many crystal-forming substances that can't be diluted in the urine, stones are formed. Avoidance of a high-fat diet can prevent gallstones while drinking a lot of water prevents kidney stones.

WHAT ARE THE FUNCTIONS OF THE LIVER?

The liver lies in the upper right part of our abdomen chiefly, above the stomach and below the diaphragm. The liver produces bile; metabolizes fats, carbohydrates and proteins; and, excretes drugs, bilirubin, cholesterol, and hormones. It makes proteins needed for blood clotting and is so important for us that we cannot live without a liver. Jaundice, cirrhosis, and liver cancer are the worst diseases of the liver.

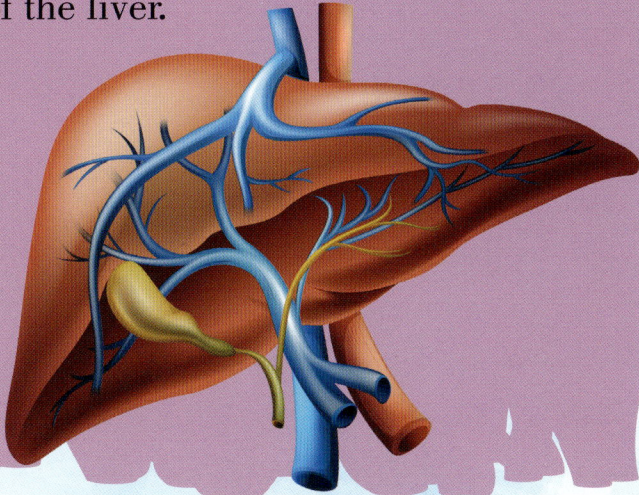

WHAT CAUSES DIABETES?

There are two main types of diabetes: type 1 and type 2. Type 1 diabetes occurs when there is a lack of insulin as the immune system destroys pancreatic cells that make insulin. Type 2 diabetes happens if the body becomes resistant to insulin, or when the pancreas doesn't make enough of it. Though diabetes can't be cured, it can go into remission with treatment, and controlling blood sugar levels.

CAN DRINKING COFFEE HELP THE BODY?

Drinking a lot of water, eating a good diet, exercising, and drinking less alcohol are factors that help the body to remain healthy. But one organ benefits from drinking coffee! As research shows, coffee is helpful to the liver, regardless of whether it is filtered, instant, or espresso! Drinking moderate amounts of coffee regularly can prevent liver cancer, lower the risk of cirrhosis, or slow the progression of the liver disease!

WHAT LEADS TO BALANCED OR SKILFUL MOVEMENT?

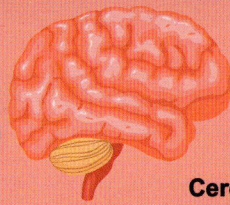

Coordination of the body muscles, joints, eyes, and the inner ear's sensory system leads to balanced movement. When the cerebellum, at the back of the brain, receives messages from these sources, it acts upon them. It's the cerebellum that controls movement and coordination, helping us to maintain our balance in sudden movements, or, perform skilfully in sports or activities such as dancing.

CEREBELLUM

Cerebrum

Corpus Callosum

Ventricles

Thalamus

Hypothalamus

Midbrain

Pituitary Gland

Cerebellum

Pons

Medulla

Brain Stem

Haemoglobin Molecule (the iron is the site of oxygen binding)

Iron

Red blood cells

Oxygen molecule

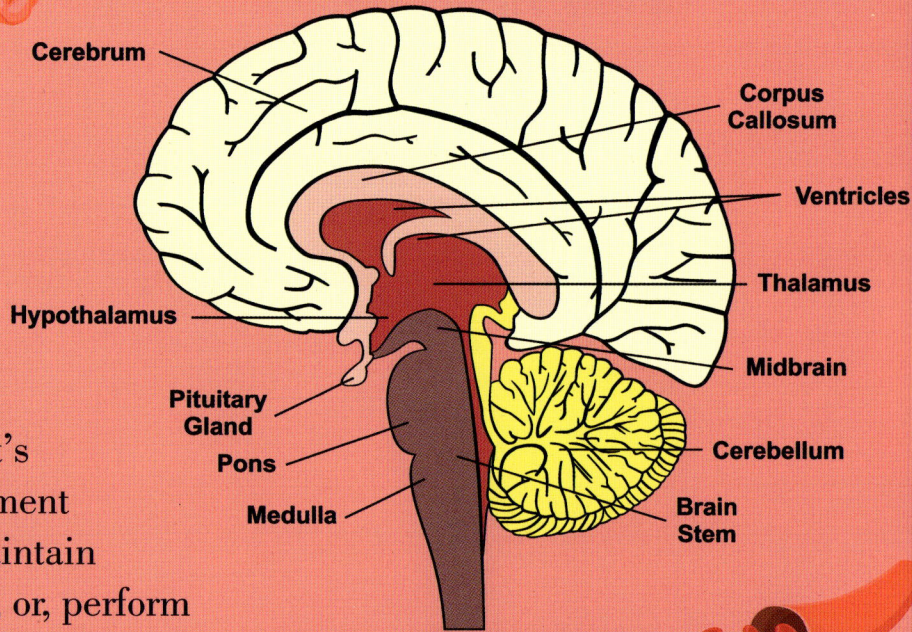

WHICH METAL ION IS PRESENT IN HAEMOGLOBIN?

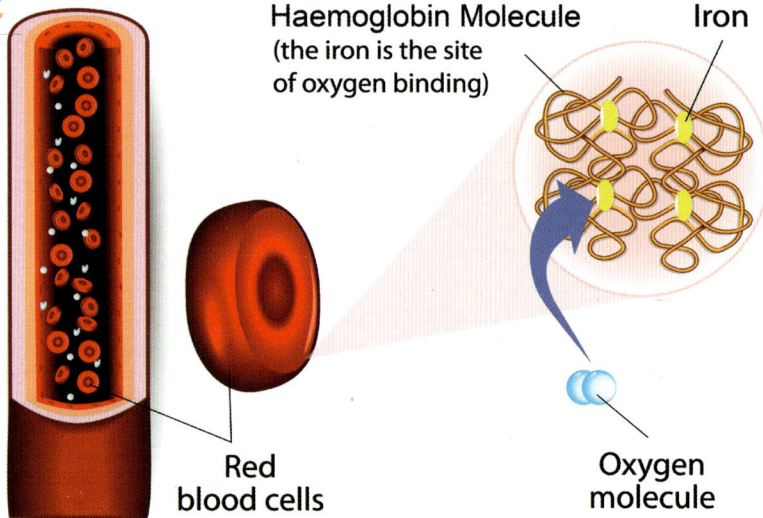

Haemoglobin is the red-coloured protein in our blood, containing iron. Oxygen is carried by the haemoglobin protein of the haem group, having iron as the central metal atom, which binds and releases molecular oxygen. Each haem group has one atom of iron, and oxygen attaches to the protein's haem part.

WHAT IS THE SCIENTIFIC NAME FOR GERMS?

Germs and microbes are called pathogens by scientists. The 4 chief types of germs are bacteria, viruses, fungi, and protozoa, which attack humans, animals, and plants. The most common diseases are spread by bacteria or viruses, and, called bacterial or viral diseases. All 4 agents of disease are called 'pathogen', coming from the Greek 'pathos' for suffering, and 'gen' for a producer.

HOW IS BLOOD PRESSURE MEASURED?

A person's blood pressure (BP) is measured with an instrument, called a sphygmomanometer. BP is measured in millimetres of mercury, or mmHg. The systolic number is recorded first, and then the diastolic number. When the heart muscle contracts in each heartbeat, oxygen-rich blood is pumped into blood vessels, making the BP rise; this gives the systolic number. When the heart muscle relaxes and is refilled with blood, the BP decreases; this is the diastolic number. The normal BP for everyone is 120/80 mm Hg.

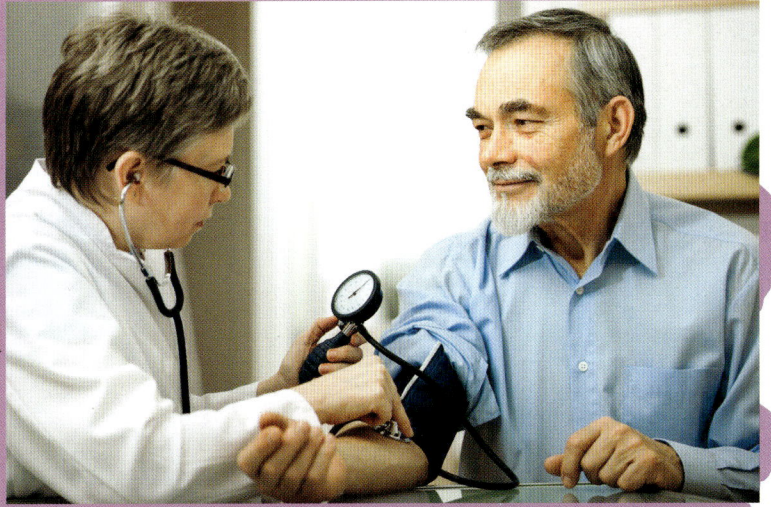

WHAT HAPPENS TO GLUCOSE INSIDE THE CELLS?

Glucose is absorbed by cells along the small intestine, from the food we eat. A glucose molecule is too big to be able to pass through a cell membrane simply. Glucose is broken down through the process of glycolysis. The energy thus released helps the cells to make adenosine triphosphate (ATP), and reduced nicotinamide adenine dinucleotide (NADH), which carries the energy to whichever part of the body needs it.

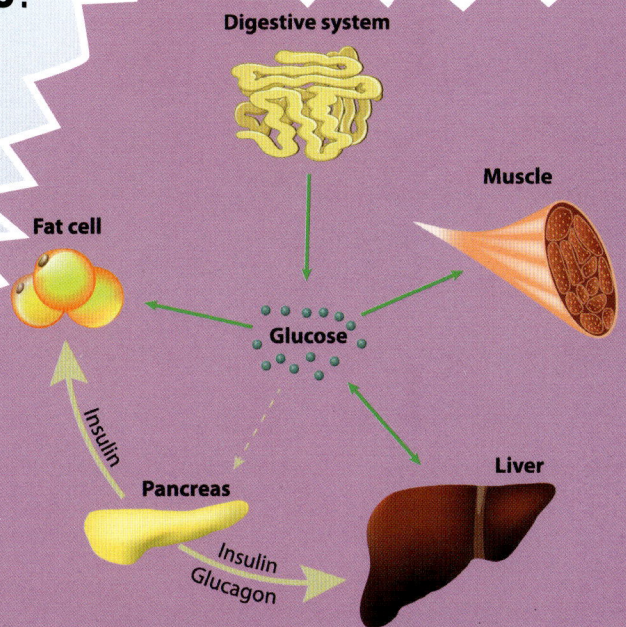

Digestive system

Muscle

Fat cell

Glucose

Insulin

Liver

Pancreas

Insulin
Glucagon

HOW THICK ARE OUR CAPILLARY WALLS?

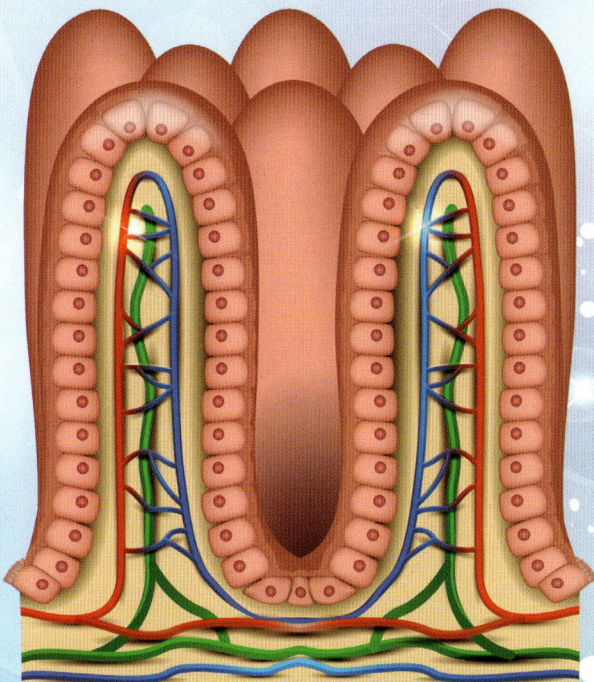

Our capillary walls are microscopic, having the thickness of just one cell. A single capillary is very tiny, allowing just a single blood cell to flow through it, at one time. The thin capillary walls permit water, oxygen, carbon dioxide, nutrients, and waste substances to be easily exchanged between the blood cells and surrounding tissues.

WHAT DO HIV AND AIDS VIRUS ATTACK IN THE HUMAN BODY?

The very dangerous HIV and AIDS virus attacks the immune system in the human body; in fact, the virus overpowers it. Once any of these diseases set in, it's impossible to reverse, and very hard to treat. In most cases, HIV and AIDS lead to death.

FITNESS DOES NOT DEPEND ON WHICH FACTOR?

If there is one thing in the body that does not affect fitness, it is height. Being tall or short has nothing to do with good health. What is needed to stay fit is a good diet and a balanced exercise regimen.

WHICH ARE THE VOLUNTARY MUSCLES?

Our body has 3 major types of muscles: skeletal, cardiac, and smooth muscles. The skeletal muscles, which are a form of striated muscle tissue, are also called voluntary muscles, as we can move them when we like. Most of these are attached to bones by tendons and found in the neck, arms, legs, or anywhere we choose to move a body part.

3 MAJOR TYPES OF MUSCLES

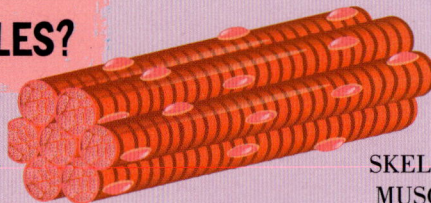

SKELETAL MUSCLES

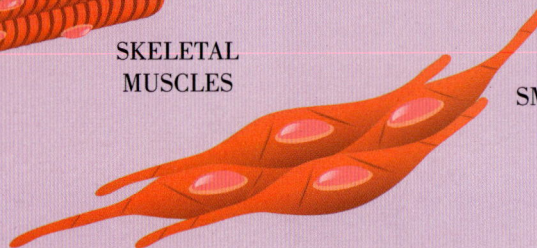

SMOOTH MUSCLES

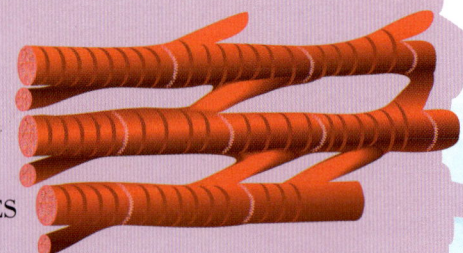

CARDIAC MUSCLES

30

Plasma is a pale yellow liquid in the blood, containing water, minerals, salts, enzymes, proteins, and antibodies. It's what is left in our blood, when red and white blood cells, platelets, and other cellular components, have been removed. It comprises around 55% of our blood, and adults usually have about 5 litres of blood.

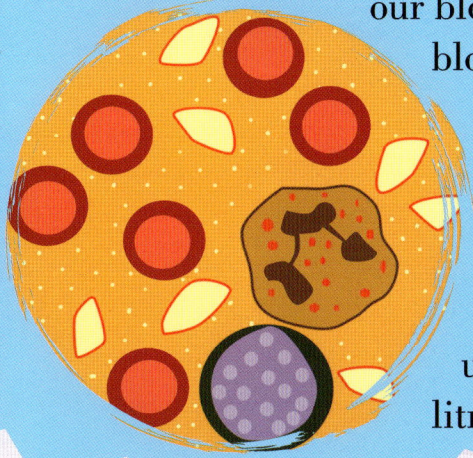

WHAT HELPS IN CLOTTING OF BLOOD?

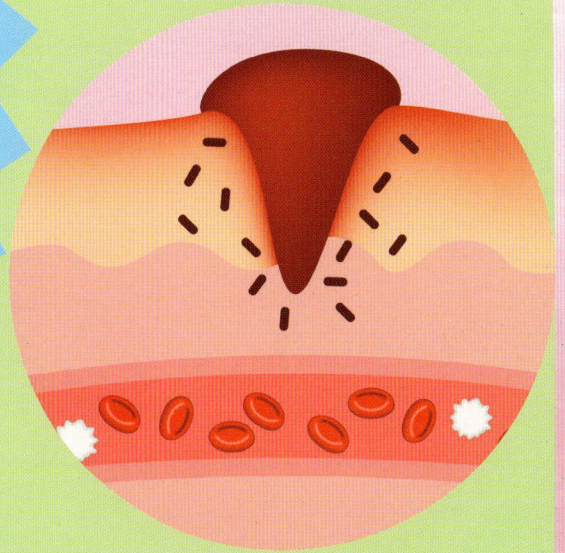

Platelets are the small blood cells, which work with proteins, to help form clots in the body, to stop bleeding. If any of the blood vessels such as veins, arteries, or capillaries get damaged, they send a signal, which is first received by the platelets. The injured spot is covered by platelets, in layers, so that further flow of blood is stopped.

WHAT ARE RESPIRATORY DISEASES?

Respiratory diseases are those that affect the lungs, nasal air passages, throat, windpipe, and bronchi. As they mainly have to do with breathing, the most common lung diseases are asthma, bronchitis, pneumonia, chronic obstructive pulmonary disease (COPD), and pulmonary fibrosis. Besides, lung cancer is a very serious disease.

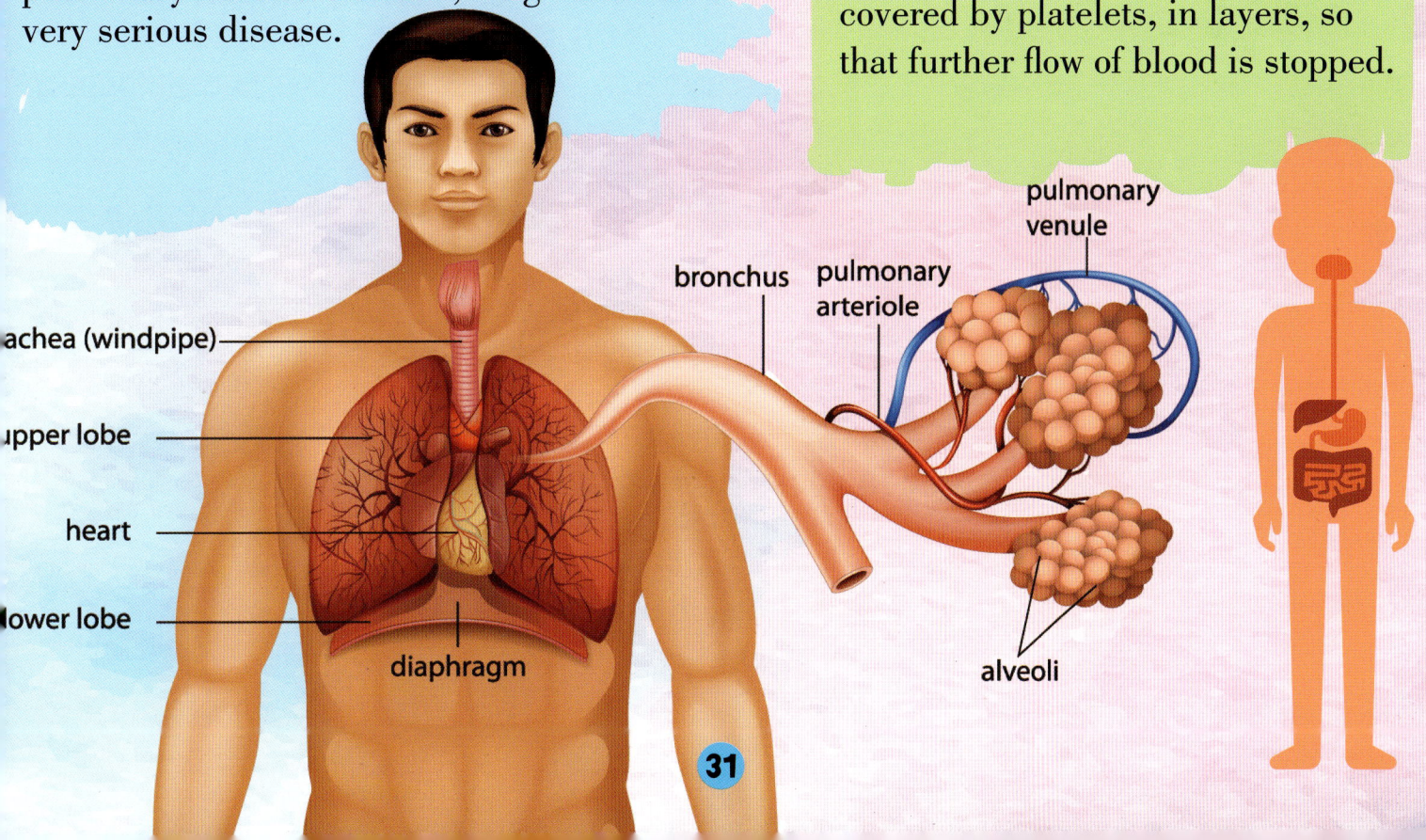

trachea (windpipe)

upper lobe

heart

lower lobe

diaphragm

bronchus

pulmonary arteriole

pulmonary venule

alveoli

WHY IS IT IMPORTANT TO STAY HYDRATED?

When about 60% of the human body is made up of water, the importance of staying hydrated can be understood. Each cell, tissue, and organ in the body requires water to function properly. Drinking water or fluids, or, eating water-rich foods helps the brain, heart, and muscles to function better. Water not only keeps the body cool but flushes out toxins, besides keeping the skin smooth and supple.

DOES THE HEART HAVE A STRONGER SIDE AND, IF SO, WHY?

The human heart does have a stronger side, and it is the left side. The left and right atria pump blood into the left and right ventricles. But the left ventricle is the bigger and thicker one, as it pumps blood to the entire body, as compared to the right ventricle.

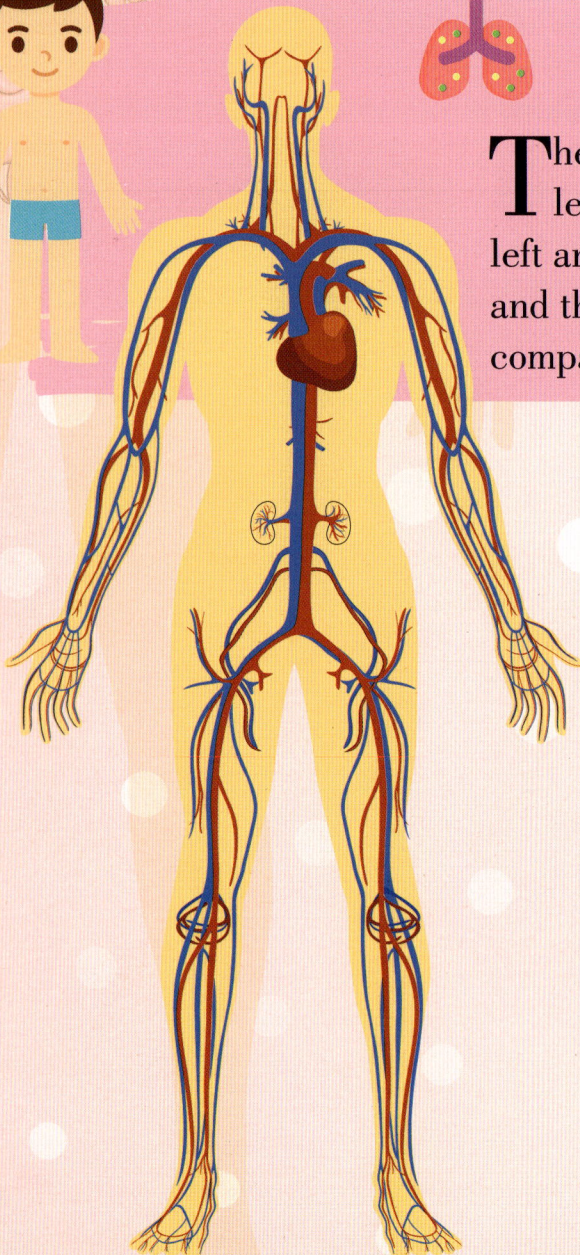

WHY ARE ENZYMES IMPORTANT FOR BODY FUNCTIONING?

Digestive enzymes break down food in the stomach and small intestine, into nutrients, so that the body can be energized, and maintain or repair bodily parts. Undigested food in the small intestine can cause various disorders, including fatigue, gastritis, arthritis, depression, ADHD (Attention deficit hyperactivity disorder), headaches, constipation, diarrhoea, thyroid problems, and more!

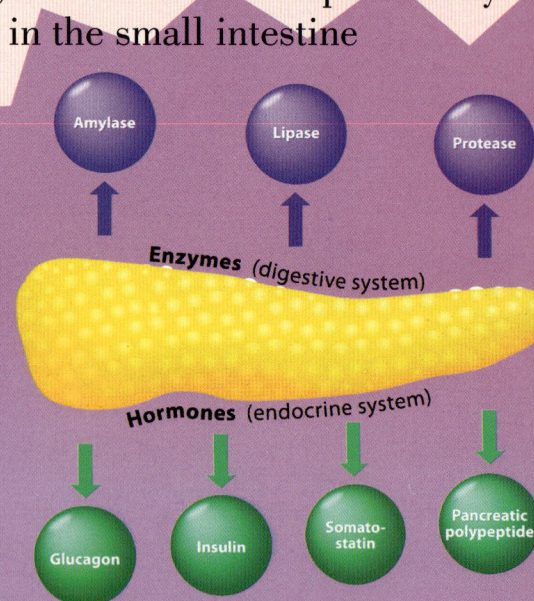

Amylase   Lipase   Protease

Enzymes (digestive system)

Hormones (endocrine system)

Glucagon   Insulin   Somato-statin   Pancreatic polypeptide

WHAT ARE ALLERGENS?

Allergens can be anything. The immune system recognizes an allergen as a dangerous element and reacts by making an antibody to fight it. This reaction causes allergy symptoms. The most common allergens are dust; pollen; animal dander; drugs, especially skin applications; fungal spores; insect stings; insect and mite faeces; natural rubber latex; and, foods, including eggs, milk, wheat, animal meat, fish, or nuts!

HOW DOES THE LYMPHATIC SYSTEM FUNCTION?

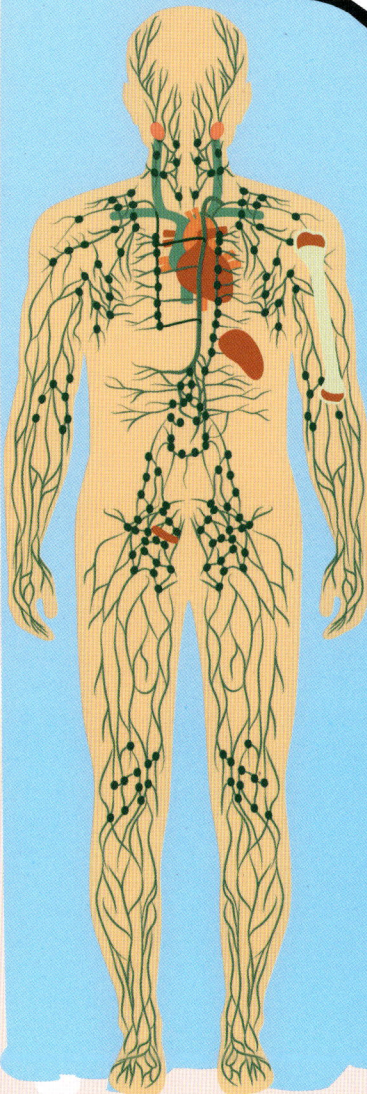

The lymphatic system contains lymph vessels, nodes, and ducts, and is part of the immune system. Lymph vessels, like blood vessels, form a network to reach out to most of the body's tissues, to circulate lymph, a clear liquid that is obtained from plasma. The key function of the lymphatic system is to protect the body from bacteria, help the body to absorb fats, and maintain the fluid balance between the tissues and blood.

WHAT IS THE TREATMENT FOR ASTHMA?

Asthma is usually triggered by an allergen. When something irritates the air passages, it causes wheezing and coughing, and can even lead to breathlessness. In some cases, the patient has to be given nebulization, which is the medicine they breathe in to clear the air passages.

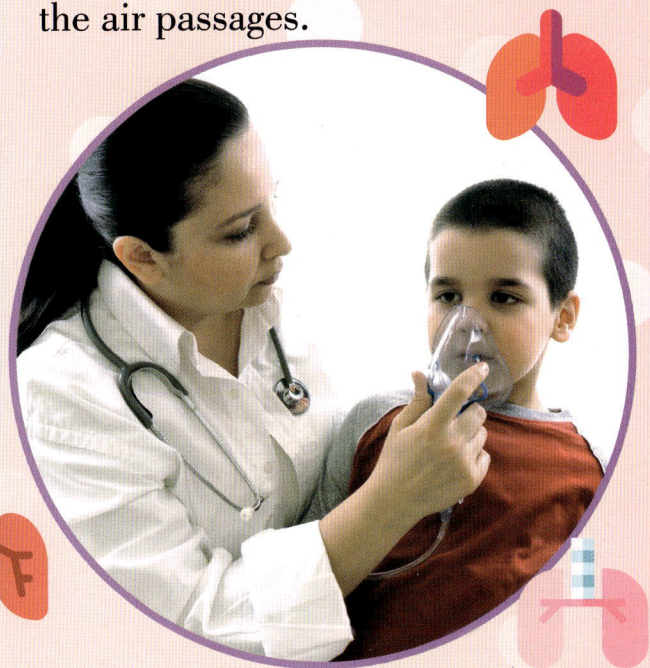

Our body has a reflex arc, which forms a neural route controlling reflex actions. On touching something very hot, we immediately withdraw our hand. But the moment we touch that hot thing, a series of events begin in the body to get the right response. Skin receptors immediately send nerve impulses through sensory neurons, not to the brain but to the spinal cord, which helps to make an immediate reflex action!

WHICH PART OF OUR BODY TRIGGERS A 'REFLEX' ACTION?

REFLEX ARC

Hot Object

Pain Receptors in Skin

Cell Body of Afferent Neuron

Axon of Afferent Neuron

Cell Body of Interneuron

Dendrite of Afferent Neuron

Axon of Efferent Neuron

Cell Body of Efferent Neuron

Spinal Cord

Direction of Impulse

Muscle Contracts and Withdraws Part Being Stimulated

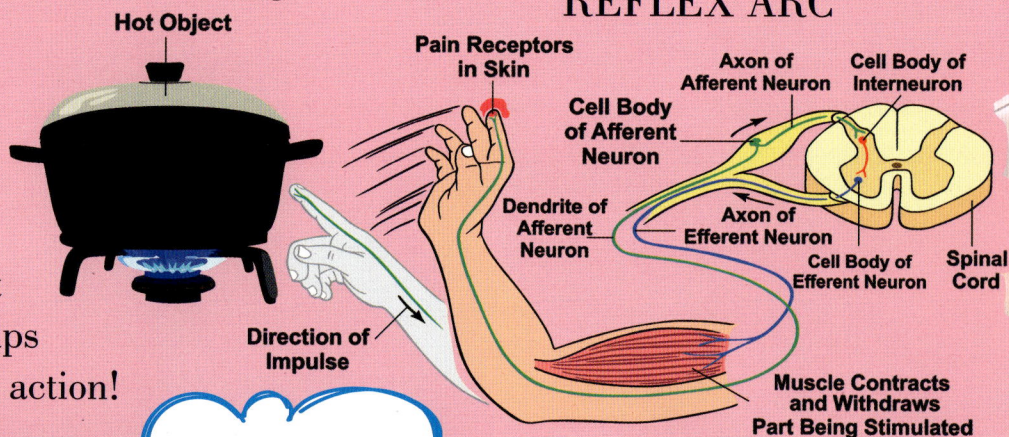

TO WHAT EXTENT IS A HEARING AID BENEFICIAL?

Hearing loss takes place when tiny hair cells, inside the inner ear, get injured or die. So, people use hearing aids, to hear what they could not hear before and, thus, communicate better over the phone or in person. But, there are unexpected side effects! Getting adjusted to hearing aids can take months, and they amplify all sounds, including one's voice, and any background noise that one may not wish to hear!

WHAT IS THE WALL OF SKIN IN THE EAR CALLED?

The eardrum is the wall of skin in the ear, which serves an important function. When sound waves enter the ear canal, they hit the thin, flexible eardrum at its end. This makes the eardrum vibrate, and the vibrations travel along the row of the ears' three small bones, to reach the cochlea. As they move, the vibrations stir rows of microscopic hair, which sends signals along the auditory nerve to the brain.

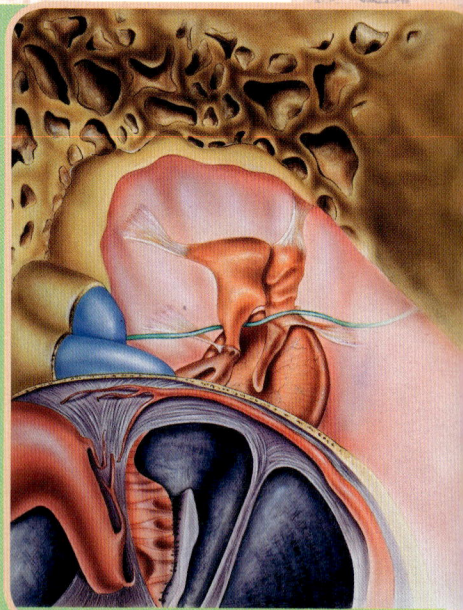

WHERE IS THE COLON FOUND?

The colon is in the large intestine, forming the final part of the digestive system. The small intestine's last part or the ileum, joins the colon's first part or cecum, in the lower right abdomen. The colon reabsorbs fluids. It also processes waste matter and prepares to get rid of it. Broccoli, dark leafy greens, milk, oatmeal, and raspberries are some of the foods that are good for the body, and the colon.

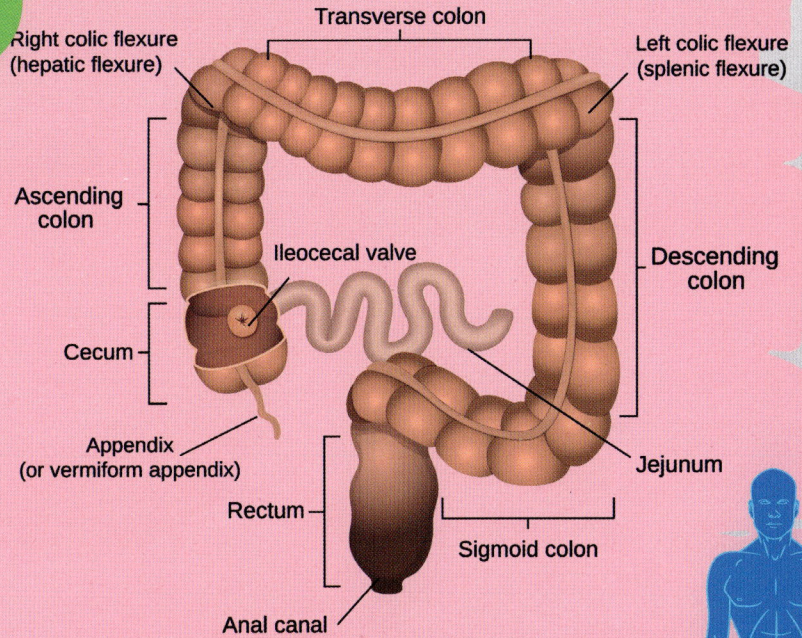

Right colic flexure (hepatic flexure)
Transverse colon
Left colic flexure (splenic flexure)
Ascending colon
Ileocecal valve
Descending colon
Cecum
Appendix (or vermiform appendix)
Jejunum
Rectum
Sigmoid colon
Anal canal

How hormones work

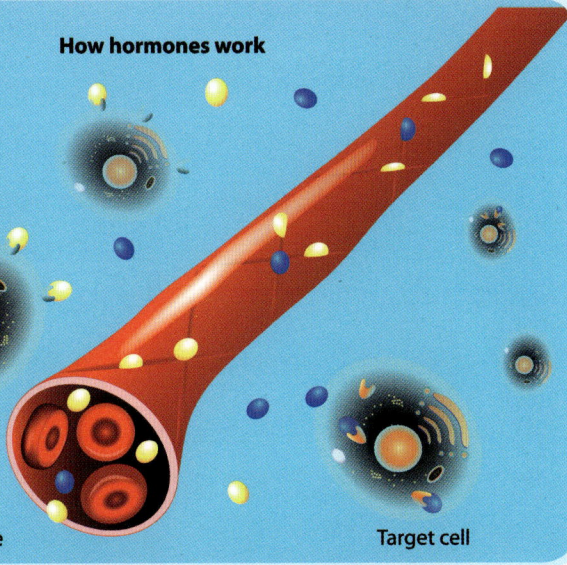

Hormone

Target cell

WHAT IS THE FUNCTION OF HORMONES?

Hormones are chemical messengers, which travel through the body to coordinate complex processes, such as growth, metabolism, and fertility. Besides, they can alter behaviour, and influence the immune system's functioning. Hormones are secreted into the blood directly, when directed by the brain, by glands of the endocrine system. There are chiefly 2 main types of hormones: those derived from amino acids, proteins, peptides, and polypeptides; and, steroid hormones.

WHICH PARTS OF OUR BODY HAVE CARTILAGE, AND CAN DAMAGED CARTILAGE REGROW?

Our body has 3 types of cartilage: Hyaline, commonly found in the nose, ribs, larynx, and trachea; Fibro, found in ligaments, joint capsules, and intervertebral discs; and, Elastic, found in the external ear, epiglottis, and larynx. Cartilage, once damaged, does not regrow easily on its own, as unlike most body tissues, it lacks a blood supply of its own. For this reason, surgeons resort to microfracture surgery to regrow cartilage.

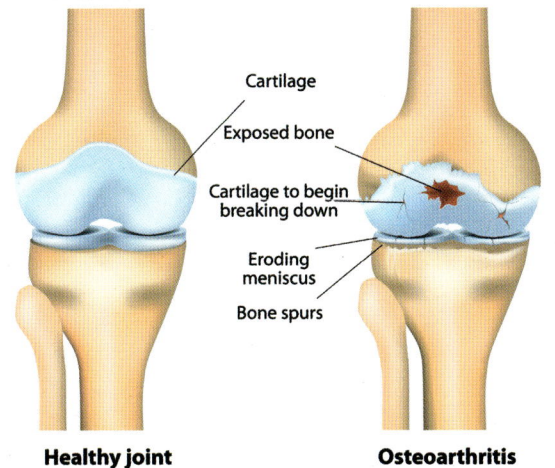

Cartilage
Exposed bone
Cartilage to begin breaking down
Eroding meniscus
Bone spurs

Healthy joint

Osteoarthritis

WHAT ARE THE LIGHT–SENSITIVE CELLS IN THE RETINA CALLED?

The retina is at the back of the eye and has cells or photoreceptors, which sense light. These are of 2 types: rods and cones. The rods are sensitive to shape and movement, and very sensitive to light and dark changes. The cones work only in bright light, but they are highly sensitive to one of three colours: red, blue, or green. But the fovea in the retina's centre, which provides the clearest vision, has only cones. The human retina has around 120 million rods and 6 million cones!

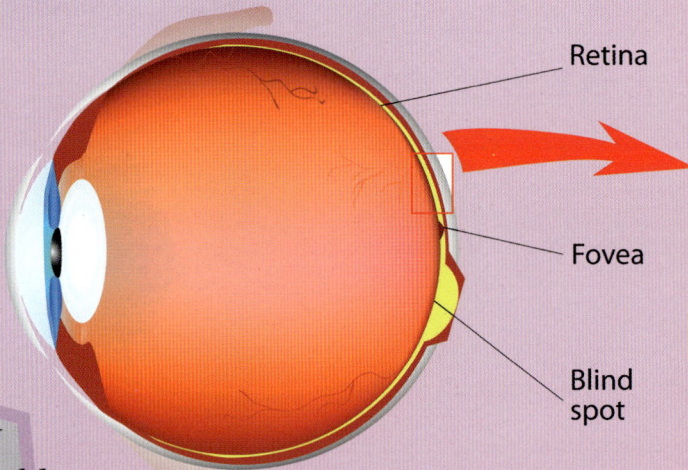

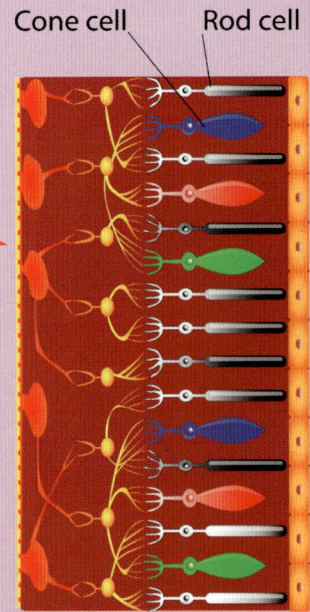

Cone cell   Rod cell

Retina

Fovea

Blind spot

WHAT IS THE CAUSE OF LONG–SIGHTEDNESS?

Long-sightedness, or hyperopia, is an eye condition in which people can see far-off objects clearly, but not those that are nearby. This happens as light entering the eye focuses behind the retina, making closer objects to be blurry, making reading difficult. People with hyperopia suffer from headaches and eye strain, and it mostly worsens with age. Options for treatment include spectacles, contact lenses, and surgery.

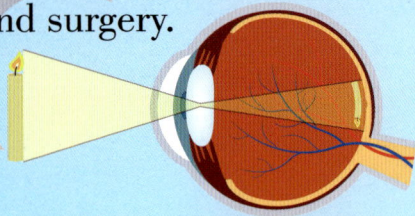

Normal vision

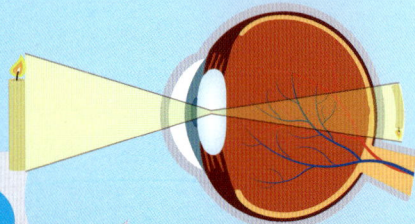

Hyperopia

WHERE IS THE HEART SITUATED?

The heart is situated in the centre of the chest, between the two lungs, and in front of the backbone. It has a slight tilt to the left. Roughly having the size of a human fist, the heart pumps blood to the entire body. It roughly weighs between 230-280 g in women, and between 280-340 g in men.

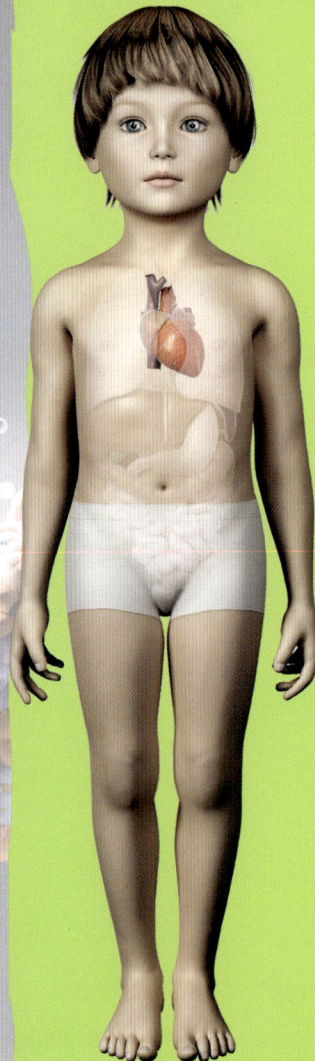

HOW DOES SMOKING HARM THE BODY?

Smoking is particularly harmful to the lungs and can lead to tuberculosis, chronic bronchitis, or cancer of the respiratory tract, and the lungs. It can set off an asthma attack, or worsen it; and, lead to a stroke or heart attack. Throat or lung cancer often requires surgery. Smoking harms not just the person who smokes, but also those around who breathe in that smoke, who are called passive smokers.

WHAT CARRIES BLOOD TO AND AWAY FROM THE HEART?

Blood is transported to and fro the whole body, through the heart's cardiovascular system of arteries and veins. Nearly all arteries circulate oxygenated or pure blood from the heart to all other parts of the body, while almost all veins bring back deoxygenated or impure blood from other bodily parts back to the heart.

FOR HOW LONG CAN A HUMAN BEING SURVIVE WITHOUT FOOD OR WATER?

Experts say that humans can survive without food for up to 60 days, but cannot survive without water for more than a week. Mahatma Gandhi survived without food for 3 weeks in 1933. Mitsutaka Uchikoshi went missing during a climbing trip in 2006, and stayed without food and water for 24 days, till found! Experts feel survival in adverse situations is an individualistic response and depends on a person's state of mind.

IS TANNING GOOD FOR THE SKIN?

People often tan themselves by basking in the sunshine. Experts advise that those who are sensitive to the sun should wear sunscreen, and stay in the sunshine for 15-30 minutes. Others believe that we should lie on our back in the sun for about 20-30 minutes, then turn over and lie on our stomach for another 20-30 minutes, to get an even suntan on the body. However, over-exposure to the sun can cause skin cancer.

WHAT ARE A BABY'S TEETH CALLED AND HOW LONG DO THEY LAST?

Babies' teeth are called milk teeth, as they look like milk, and are whiter than adult teeth. Also called primary or deciduous teeth, baby teeth start to form before a baby is born, but usually pierce through the skin when the baby is between 6-12 months old. Most children have their full set of 20 teeth by the age of 3 years. Between the ages of 5-6, the milk teeth start falling out at various times, making way for adult teeth.

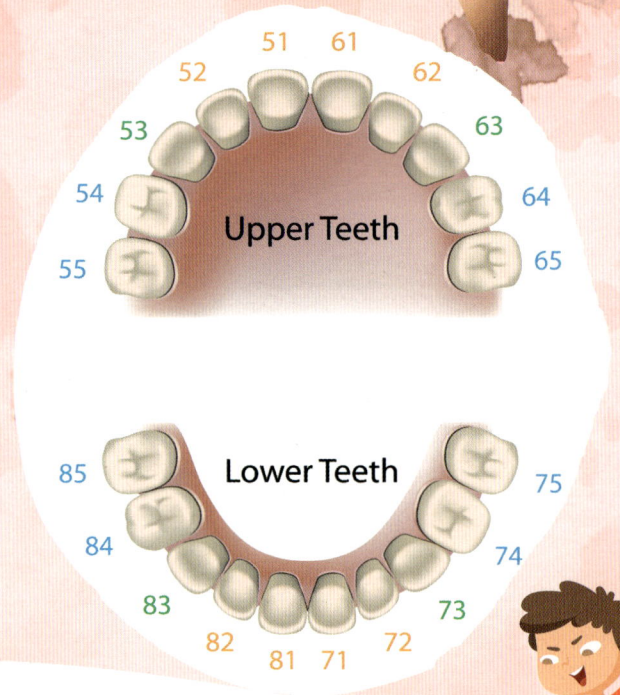

Upper Teeth

51 61
52   62
53   63
54   64
55   65

Lower Teeth

85   75
84   74
83   73
82 81 71 72

WHY ARE SOME CHILDREN HYPERACTIVE?

Children are usually active by nature, but some are hyperactive. They try to do various things at the same time, are fidgety, lack focus, refuse to play quietly, jump from one activity to another, are inattentive, or are unable to control their impulses. This is a sign of attention deficit hyperactivity disorder (ADHD). Only about 33% of children outgrow ADHD during adolescence, but the rest have it even as adults.

38

WHY DOES VOMIT TASTE SOUR?

People who suffer from acid reflux often have a sour taste in the mouth due to stomach acids. At times, acid backs up in the throat or mouth, leaving a sour or bitter taste. Frequent burping, coughing, heartburn, or indigestion, as in reflux and gastroesophageal reflux disease (GERD), can cause nausea or vomiting, with vomit tasting sour. Eating bananas, melons, oatmeal, green vegetables, and yogurt can get rid of acid reflux.

DOES EVERYONE HAVE THE SAME TYPE OF SKIN?

People can have any of 4 different types of skin: dry, oily, normal, and combination. Still, others can have sensitive skin, which may be too dry, red, or, have burning or itching. What's more, skin type can change over the years! But, whatever the skin type, if people avoid direct sunlight and smoking, drink enough water, wash skin thoroughly each day, and use a moisturizer, their skin will look its best.

WHAT IS OUR SKIN MADE UP OF?

Our skin is made up of 3 layers. The epidermis is what we see, below it is the dermis, and deep down is the subcutis. The epidermis consists of dead cells but keeps growing new cells. The dermis has a thick network of elastic collagen fibres and capillaries. The subcutis is chiefly made up of connective tissue and fats. Both the bottom layers have blood and lymph vessels, nerves, scent and oil glands, and hair roots.

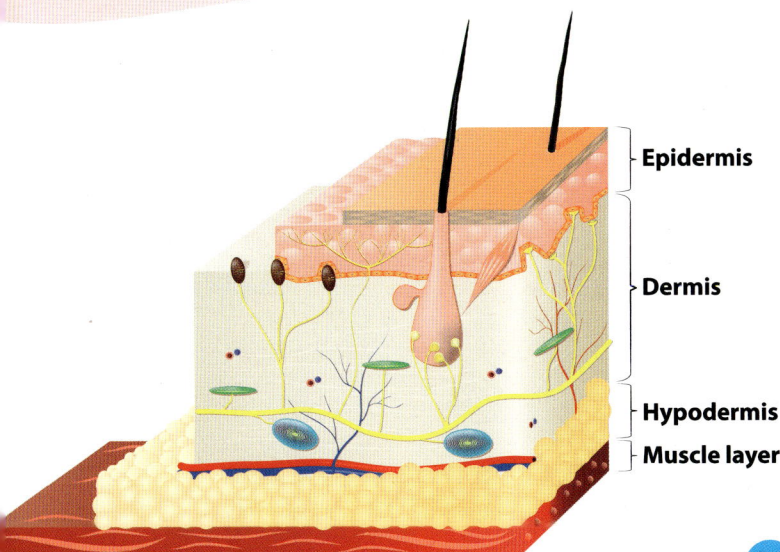

Epidermis

Dermis

Hypodermis

Muscle layer

39

WHAT CAUSES LEUKAEMIA?

Leukaemia is a fatal blood cancer. It happens when the bone marrow makes an enormous amount of abnormal white blood cells, which attack the body's immune system instead of defending it. There's no obvious cause of this disease though doctors try to treat it. Research suggests that a good diet may help, including 10 fruits and vegetables a day, whole grains and legumes, and fish, lean meats, and poultry.

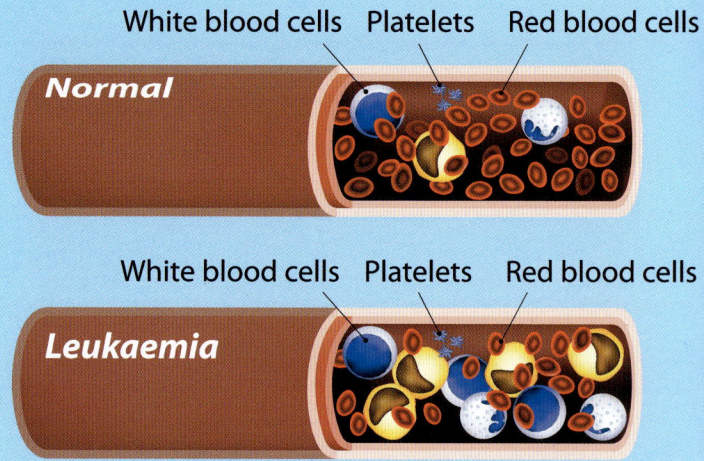

White blood cells   Platelets   Red blood cells

Normal

White blood cells   Platelets   Red blood cells

Leukaemia

3 MAJOR TYPES OF MUSCLES

SKELETAL MUSCLES

SMOOTH MUSCLES

CARDIAC MUSCLES

IN WHICH PART OF THE BODY IS OUR BIGGEST MUSCLE?

We have 3 types of muscle tissue: skeletal, smooth, and cardiac. One of the over 600 skeletal muscles performing different tasks, and the largest muscle by volume, is the Gluteus Maximus. Along with the other gluteal muscles, Gluteus Maximus stabilizes the lower back and pelvis to enable an upright posture; and is the chief antigravity muscle as it helps in climbing stairs and sitting, besides walking and running.

WHICH MINERAL IS GOOD FOR BONES?

Calcium is the most important mineral for healthy bones. Besides, bones also need a constant supply and a good amount of vitamin D, magnesium, and vitamin K2 for bone density and health. Bones also require trace minerals for their growth, though in lesser amounts. These trace minerals include strontium, silicon, vanadium, copper, etc.

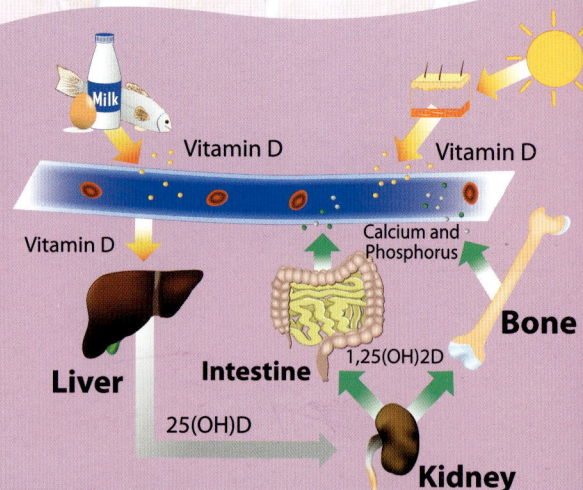

Vitamin D

Vitamin D

Vitamin D

Calcium and Phosphorus

Bone

Liver

Intestine

1,25(OH)2D

25(OH)D

Kidney

WHAT IS THE COLOUR OF HEALTHY BONES, AND WHAT IS THE COLOUR OF THE MARROW IN THEM?

In living people, bones are grey and active. They contain blood vessels that bring nourishment, and nerves that feel pressure and pain. When bones have been dead for long, they become white and brittle. Red marrow, present mainly in flat bones, such as the pelvis or hip bone, makes more than 2 million new blood cells every second! While yellow marrow in the other bones, stores fat that can be turned into energy.

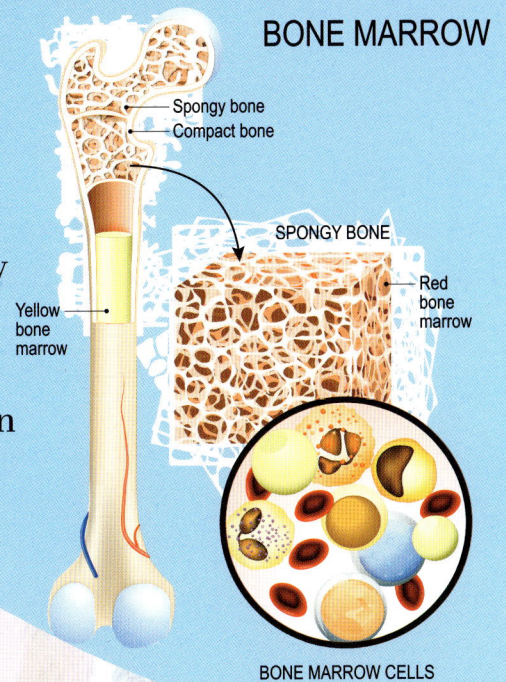

BONE MARROW

Spongy bone
Compact bone

SPONGY BONE

Red bone marrow

Yellow bone marrow

BONE MARROW CELLS

WHY DO WE GET PIMPLES?

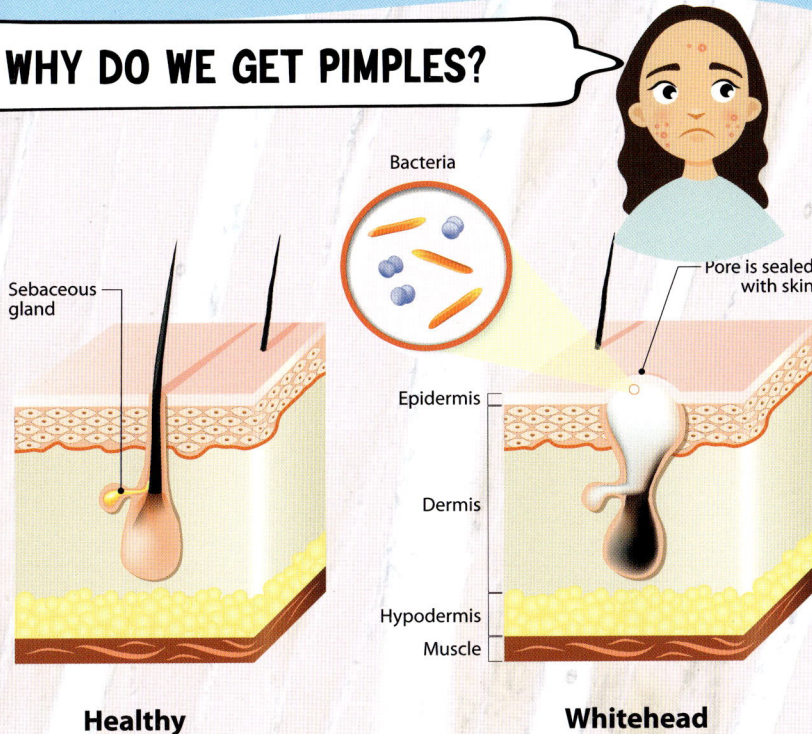

Bacteria

Pore is sealed with skin

Sebaceous gland

Epidermis

Dermis

Hypodermis

Muscle

Healthy

Whitehead

Pimples are tiny oil-filled bumps on the face. People having oily skin are most likely to be affected. Hair follicles or pores in the skin, contain oil or sebaceous glands. These produce sebum, which lubricates the skin and hair. When too much sebum is produced, the pores get clogged. Bacteria gets trapped in the pores, and begins to multiply, which is the beginning of pimples, and even acne.

HOW DO BLACKHEADS FORM?

Like pimples, blackheads appear on the face, as the result of overactive sebaceous glands. Each hair follicle contains a sebaceous gland and one hair. When oil, dead skin cells or keratin, and bacteria accumulate in the follicle's opening, the pore turns into a bump or comedo. What comes out of a blackhead is chiefly keratin and sebum, which darkens as due to exposure to air; the rest of it is creamy or yellowish.

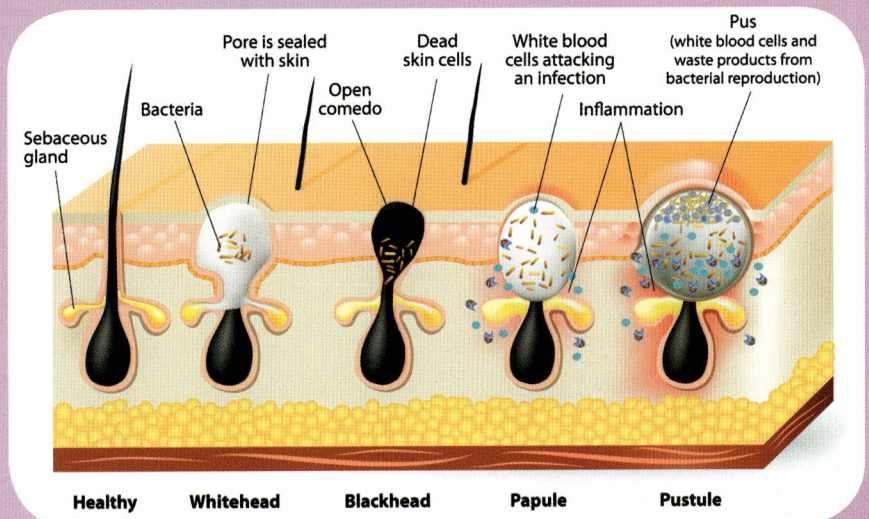

Pus (white blood cells and waste products from bacterial reproduction)

Pore is sealed with skin

Dead skin cells

White blood cells attacking an infection

Open comedo

Inflammation

Bacteria

Sebaceous gland

Healthy   **Whitehead**   **Blackhead**   **Papule**   **Pustule**

WHAT IS THE FUNCTION OF BONE MARROW?

Bone marrow, which is red and yellow, is the flexible, soft, connective tissue, located in bone cavities. Red marrow produces red and white blood cells, and platelets; while yellow marrow chiefly contains fat cells. Till early childhood, most of the marrow is red. More yellow marrow is formed as people grow. In adults around half their bone marrow is red. Bone marrow transplants have been done to treat acute diseases of bone marrow as in cancer, particularly leukaemia.

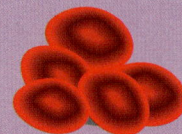

Platelets

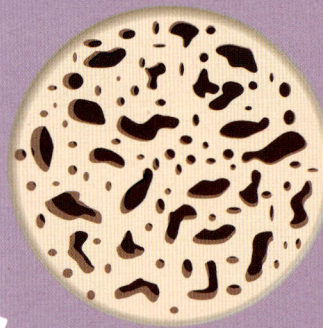

Bone marrow

Red blood cells

White blood cells

WHAT DO WE BREATHE IN AND OUT?

What we breathe in is not pure oxygen. The air we breathe in contains 21% oxygen only; with 78% nitrogen; 0.965% argon; and, 0.04% carbon dioxide besides some helium, other gases, and water vapour. What we breathe out contains just 4% carbon dioxide; 78% nitrogen; around 16% oxygen; 0.96% argon, other gases, and water vapour.

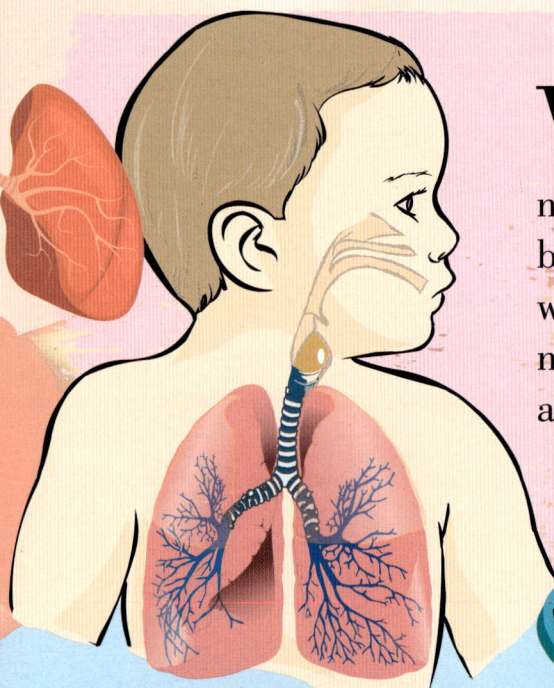

WHAT IS ACNE?

Acne is a skin ailment, appearing as blackheads, whiteheads, pimples, nodules, cysts, or skin lesions, which show up on the face, neck, shoulders, chest, and stomach. It can happen to females and males of all ages. Skin applications can get rid of acne, but a dermatologist can decide best what treatment should be taken.

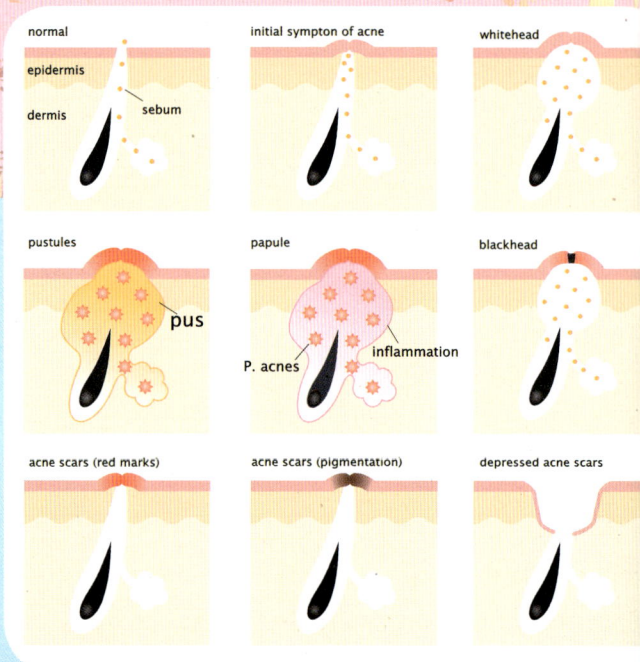

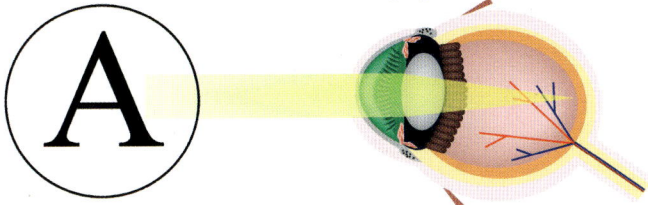
Vision in a healthy eye

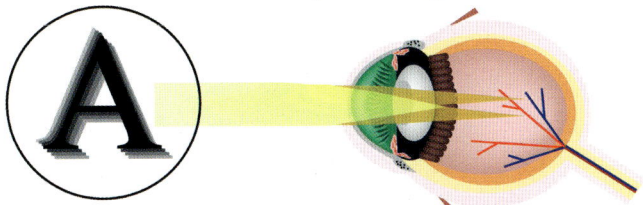
The vision in the eye with astigmatism

WHAT IS ASTIGMATISM?

A vision problem occurs when the shape of the eye's lens or cornea develops an irregular curve. This is a common problem, called astigmatism. It changes the way in which light passes to the retina, and can cause distorted, fuzzy, or blurry vision. However, the problem can be corrected with contact lenses, spectacles, or surgery.

WHAT CAUSES A BLIND SPOT IN THE EYE?

In each eye of humans, there is a natural blind spot. These correspond to the position of the optic nerve head, or optic disk, in the retina. There are no photoreceptors in this area, so no images are detected here. Clinical evaluation of the optic nerve head is crucial in the detection and monitoring of glaucoma, or other eye-related disorders, which may cause vision loss.

GLAUCOMA

damage to optic nerve

abnormal pressure inside eye

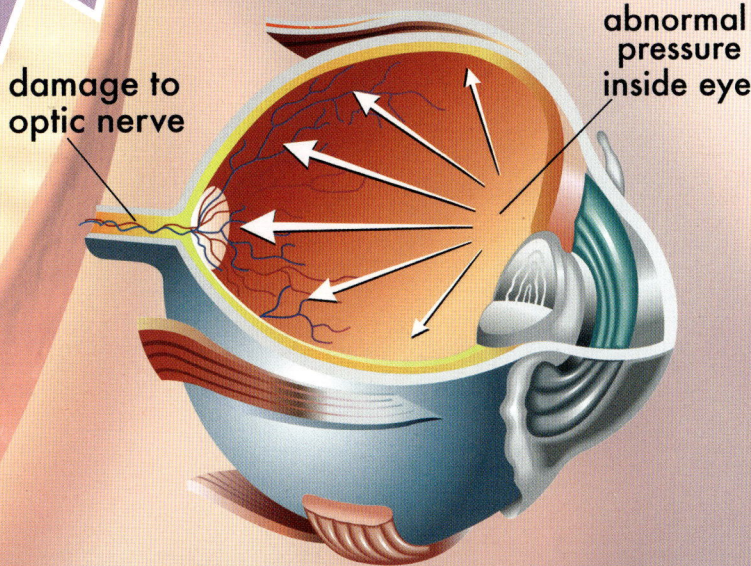

WHAT CAUSES SHORT–SIGHTEDNESS?

Short-sightedness or near-sightedness, also called myopia, is an eye disorder in which light focuses in front of the retina, instead of on it. It mostly occurs when the eyeball grows a little too long. In this condition, objects that are near can be seen clearly, while those at a distance appear blurred. It can be a mild disorder or significantly impair vision, but can be corrected by using spectacles, contact lenses, or surgery.

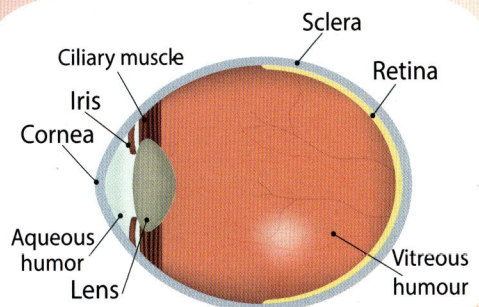
Myopia

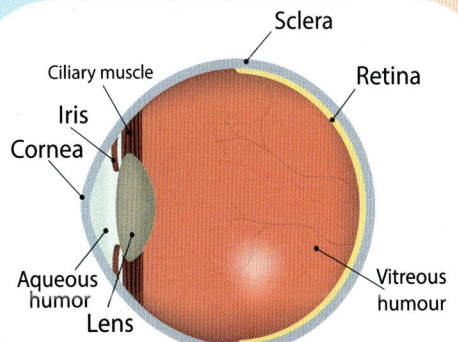
Normal

WHICH IS THE LONGEST CELL IN THE HUMAN BODY?

The human body has many long cells, which are nerve cells, or neurons. Part of the nervous system, these neurons carry messages through the body. The axon or nerve fibre is a long, thin projection of a neuron, conducting electrical impulses, and the longest axons are those of the sciatic nerve. These run from the spinal cord's base to the big toe in each foot.

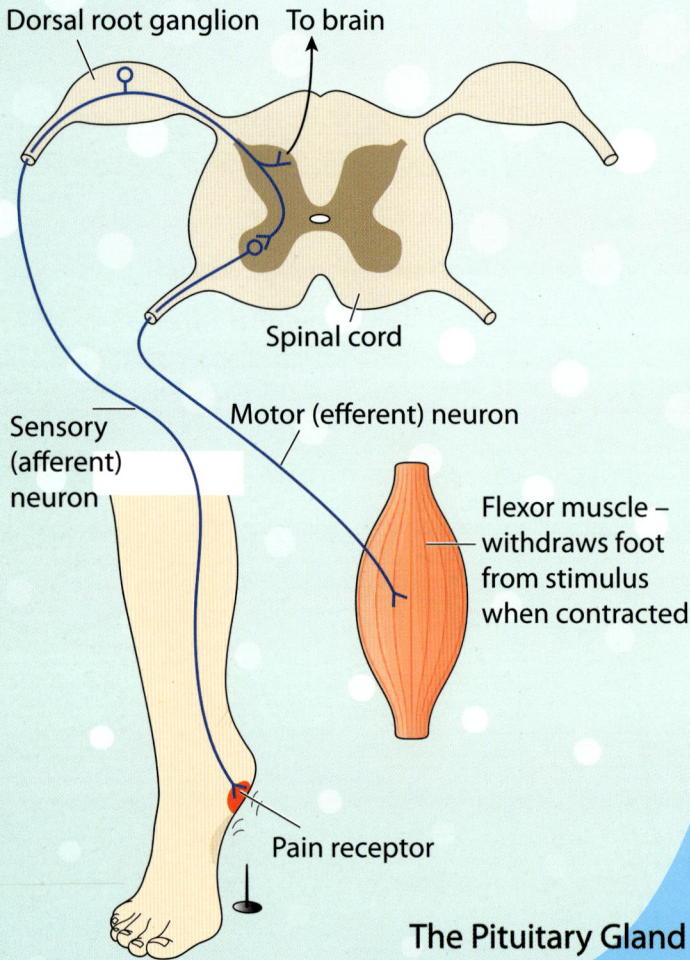

Dorsal root ganglion   To brain

Spinal cord

Sensory (afferent) neuron

Motor (efferent) neuron

Flexor muscle – withdraws foot from stimulus when contracted

Pain receptor

HOW MANY PAIRS OF SPINAL NERVES ARE THERE IN OUR BODY?

All vertebrates have spinal nerves, which are paired peripheral nerves arising from the spinal cord. Every nerve pair joins the spinal cord to a particular body region. Human beings have 31 pairs of spinal nerves. These are 8 cervical, 1 coccygeal, 5 sacral, 5 lumbar, and 12 thoracics.

WHICH GLANDS DECREASE IN SIZE, AS HUMAN BEINGS GROW OLDER?

As human beings grow older, certain changes take place in their bodies. The sweat glands shrink, particularly under the arms, and produce less perspiration. The pituitary gland, which is in the brain, and is part of the endocrine system, starts reducing gradually after middle age.

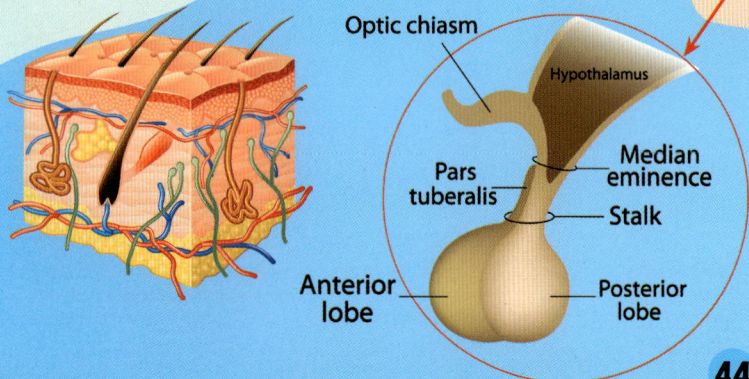

The Pituitary Gland

Optic chiasm

Hypothalamus

Pars tuberalis

Median eminence

Stalk

Anterior lobe

Posterior lobe

HOW WAS BRAILLE INVENTED?

Braille is a system of touch reading, meant for the visually impaired, using fingers, with raised dots representing the letters of the alphabet. It was invented by Louis Braille in the 19th century, who lost his vision early in life. He was studying at the Royal Institution for Blind Youth, when Charles Barbier, a captain from Napoleon's army introduced the system of writing with dots and dashes, used by soldiers to communicate without speaking! And this led to Louis formulating a language that was given his name – Braille.

BRAILLE Alphabet

A B C D E F G H I
J K L M N O P Q R
S T U V W X Y Z
. , ? ! ' ' - CAPITAL # 0
1 2 3 4 5 6 7 8 9

CAN WE SMELL UNDERWATER?

It's not possible to smell underwater. When humans, and most other mammalian creatures, dive underwater, they cannot smell anything, as it's impossible to inhale without gulping water! But, some aquatic creatures, such as lobsters, water shrew, and star-nosed mole are able to sniff out food sources underwater!

WHAT IS THE QUIETEST SOUND WE CAN HEAR?

The quietest sound we can hear is the sound of a pin falling to the ground; referred to as a pin drop silence! Technically, the threshold of hearing is referred to as RMS sound pressure of 20 micro pascals, which corresponds to a sound intensity of 0.98 pW/m2 at 1 atmosphere and 25°C. This is the quietest sound humans with good hearing can detect at 1,000 Hz.

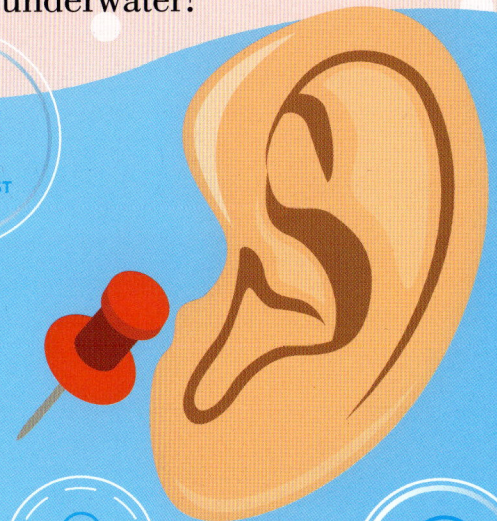

TINNITUS

HEARING TEST

HEARING AIDS

AUDITORY

WHICH SIDE OF OUR TONGUE RESPONDS TO A BITTER TASTE?

In 1901, German scientist David P Hanig made a line graph to show that the tongue has sweet receptors in the front, sour and salty along the sides, and bitter at the back. Based on this, in the 1940s, Dr Boring, brought out a tongue map, showing that different tastes are felt by different parts of the tongue. Many researchers proved it wrong in the following decades, establishing that the tongue's receptors respond equally to various tastes all over the tongue. Though the edges and tips of the tongue are more sensitive to taste, as they have taste buds.

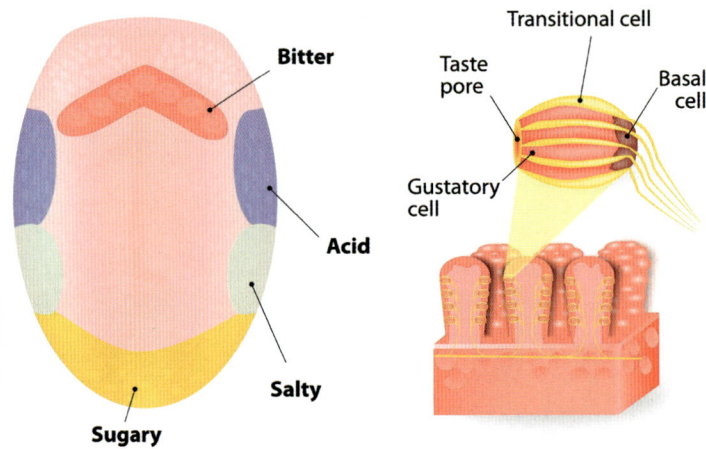

Bitter

Acid

Salty

Sugary

Transitional cell

Taste pore

Basal cell

Gustatory cell

HOW DOES THE BRAIN FUNCTION?

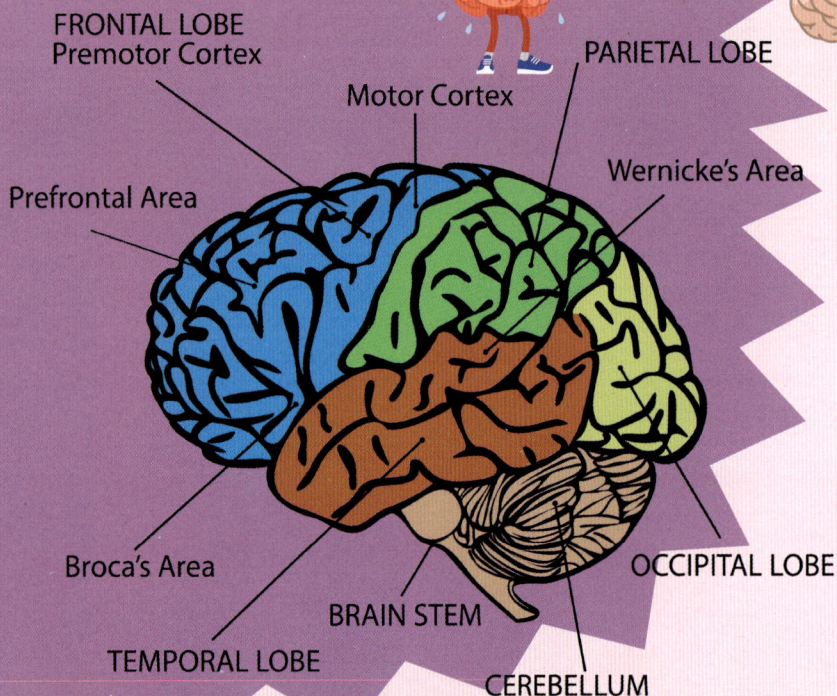

The human brain is a mass of white and grey matter, weighing 3 pounds. This very complex organ influences all our activities. Even when the body sleeps, the brain does not! The brain is composed of billions of cells, or neurons, which are organized into networks and circuits. When a neuron receives a sufficient number of messages from other group neurons, then it sends the message on to other neurons in its network!

FRONTAL LOBE
Premotor Cortex

Motor Cortex

PARIETAL LOBE

Prefrontal Area

Wernicke's Area

Broca's Area

OCCIPITAL LOBE

BRAIN STEM

TEMPORAL LOBE

CEREBELLUM

WHAT KEEPS ON GROWING ALL THROUGH A HUMAN BEING'S LIFE?

Humans normally stop growing at the onset of adulthood. But, our nose and ears, which are made up of cartilage, grow throughout life. In 1995, a study established that men's ears had grown longer by 0.22 mm in a year. The reason is that cartilage keeps growing, so our ears and nose also grow.

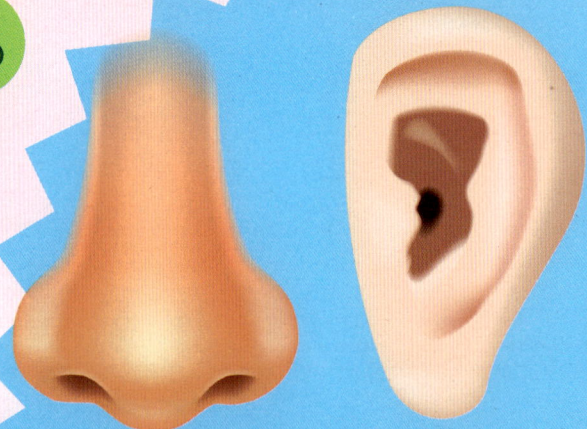

WHAT IS THE CAUSE OF ANXIETY, AND HOW CAN IT BE TREATED?

A Worry or stress causes anxiety, but it's believed that anxiety disorders may be linked to chemical imbalances in the brain. If chronic anxiety is left untreated, it can worsen certain major psychiatric disorders. A lack of vitamins and minerals is linked to mood disorders, anxiety, and depression. Vitamin B is seen as a natural anti-depressant, especially folic acid or vitamin B-9, with other vitamins of the B group.

WHAT IS THE ROLE OF CHEMICALS IN THE BRAIN?

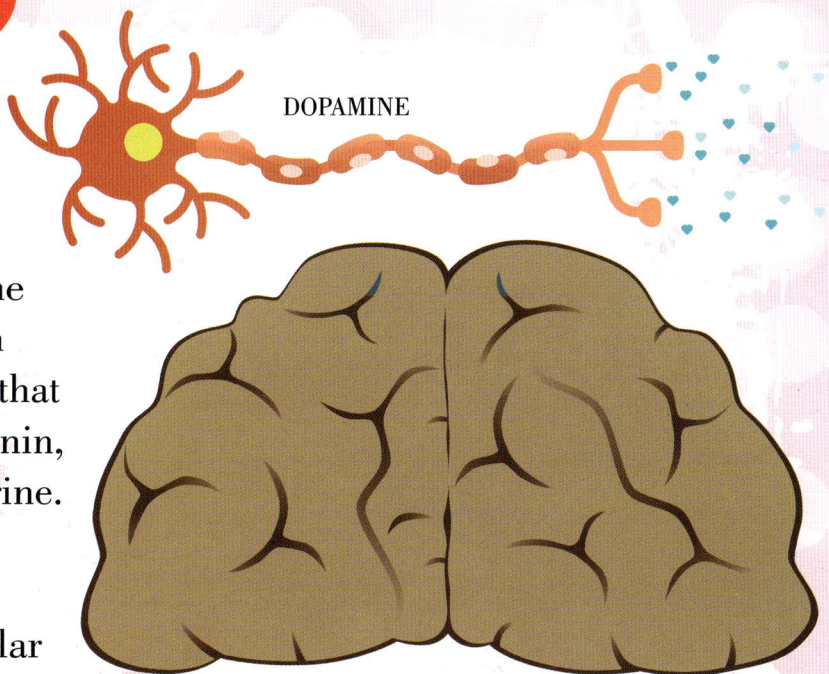

DOPAMINE

The brain transmits messages from one neuron, or nerve, to another, through chemicals. There are 4 main chemicals that greatly affect mood and thinking: Serotonin, Dopamine, Glutamate, and Norepinephrine. A low level or an imbalance of these neurotransmitter chemicals can lead to serious conditions, such as autism, bipolar disorder, depression, schizophrenia, or Parkinson's disease.

WHICH PARTS OF THE BRAIN ARE AFFECTED BY USAGE OF DRUGS?

Usage of drugs can alter 3 vital areas of the brain. The basal ganglia motivate us positively and make us feel the pleasurable effects of eating and socializing. The extended amygdala heightens feelings of anxiety, stress, or irritation, and makes us want to use a drug again. The pre-frontal cortex helps people to think, plan, and take decisions, but its powers of self-restraint are eroded if one doesn't stop taking drugs.

HOW DOES INTAKE OF SUGAR HELP US?

Our body needs carbohydrates to provide us energy, for which the body breaks them down into sugar. Simple sugars, such as table sugar and honey, cause quick drops and spikes in blood sugar. Complex carbohydrates as in grains, cereals, bread, and starchy vegetables take longer to digest, but provide sustained energy and have steadier blood sugar levels. But excessive sugar intake can lead to obesity, diabetes, heart disease, insomnia, or low energy.

WHY DOES BLOOD APPEAR RED?

Blood carries haemoglobin, which is a red-coloured protein, containing iron. Haemoglobin is produced by erythrocytes or red blood cells, in the bone marrow, and is found in the blood within them. Each haemoglobin is made up of haems, which can bind iron molecules and which, in turn, bind oxygen. The blood cells become red, due to the interaction between oxygen and iron.

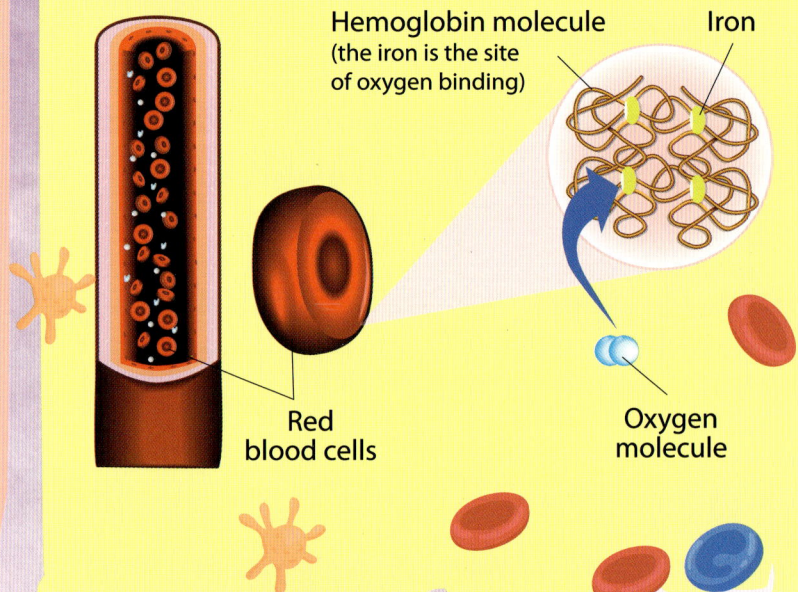

Hemoglobin molecule (the iron is the site of oxygen binding)

Iron

Red blood cells

Oxygen molecule

WHAT DO THE ARTERIES CONTAIN?

We know that arteries carry rich, oxygenated blood, from the heart and distribute it to other body parts. However, they also contain something that can be very harmful. Sometimes, cholesterol, calcium, fat, and other substances in the blood, harden to form plaque inside the arteries. Over time, the arteries become narrow and are unable to distribute blood fully to the body. This disease is called Atherosclerosis, which can cause a heart attack, stroke, or death.

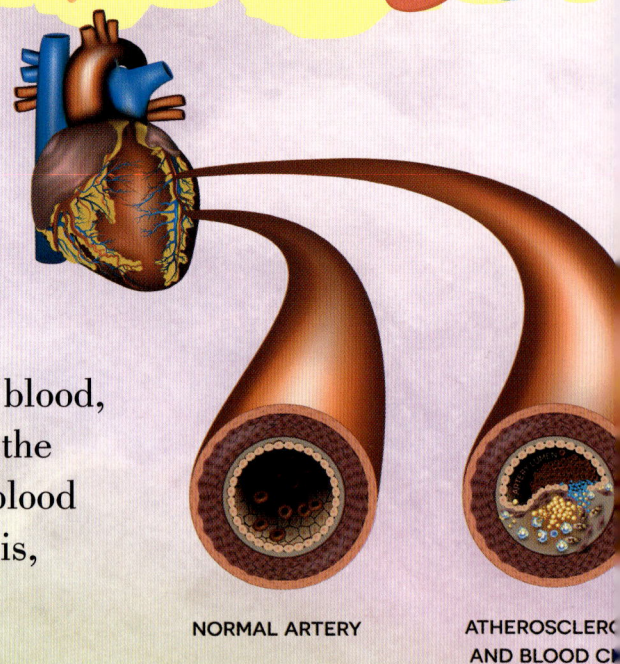

NORMAL ARTERY

ATHEROSCLERO AND BLOOD C

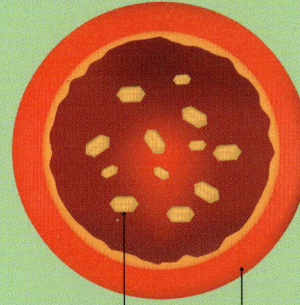

WHAT IS HYPERGLYCEMIA?

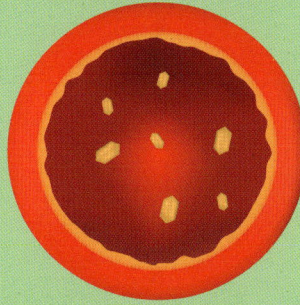

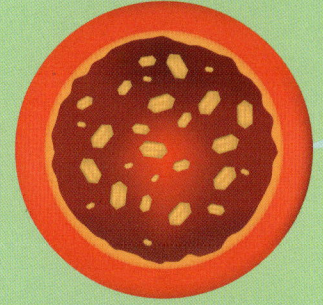

Hyperglycemia is a sugar-related disorder, in which excess sugar in the blood can cause diabetes. High levels of blood sugar, fatigue, weight loss, frequent urination, and blurred vision are some of its signs. Regular exercise, keeping correct blood sugar levels, and adjusting insulin doses, can keep hyperglycemia under control.

Hypoglycemia   **Normal**   **Hyperglycemia**

Glucose   Blood vessel

WHAT IS THE TIBIA, AND WHERE IS LOCATED?

The tibia also called the shinbone, is the bigger and stronger of the two bones, in the lower front portion of the leg. It connects the knee to the ankle bones, and is the second-largest bone, next to the femur. The other bone in this area is the fibula or calf bone. The tibia is connected through its entire length to the fibula, by the interosseous membrane. The leg bones, including the femur, tibia, and fibula are the toughest long bones, as they carry the weight of the rest of the body.

Femur

Cartilage

Patella (Knee Cap)

Synovia

Tibia

Fibulae

HOW CAN WE PRACTICE DENTAL HYGIENE AT HOME?

It's important to practice dental hygiene at home so that we can save our teeth from developing caries or plaque, and keep them shining white. To this end, dentists recommend that we brush our teeth twice daily and especially before going to bed, clean between the teeth, eat a healthy diet by limiting sugary beverages and snacks, and regularly visit a dentist, who can give the best advice for any dental problem.

49

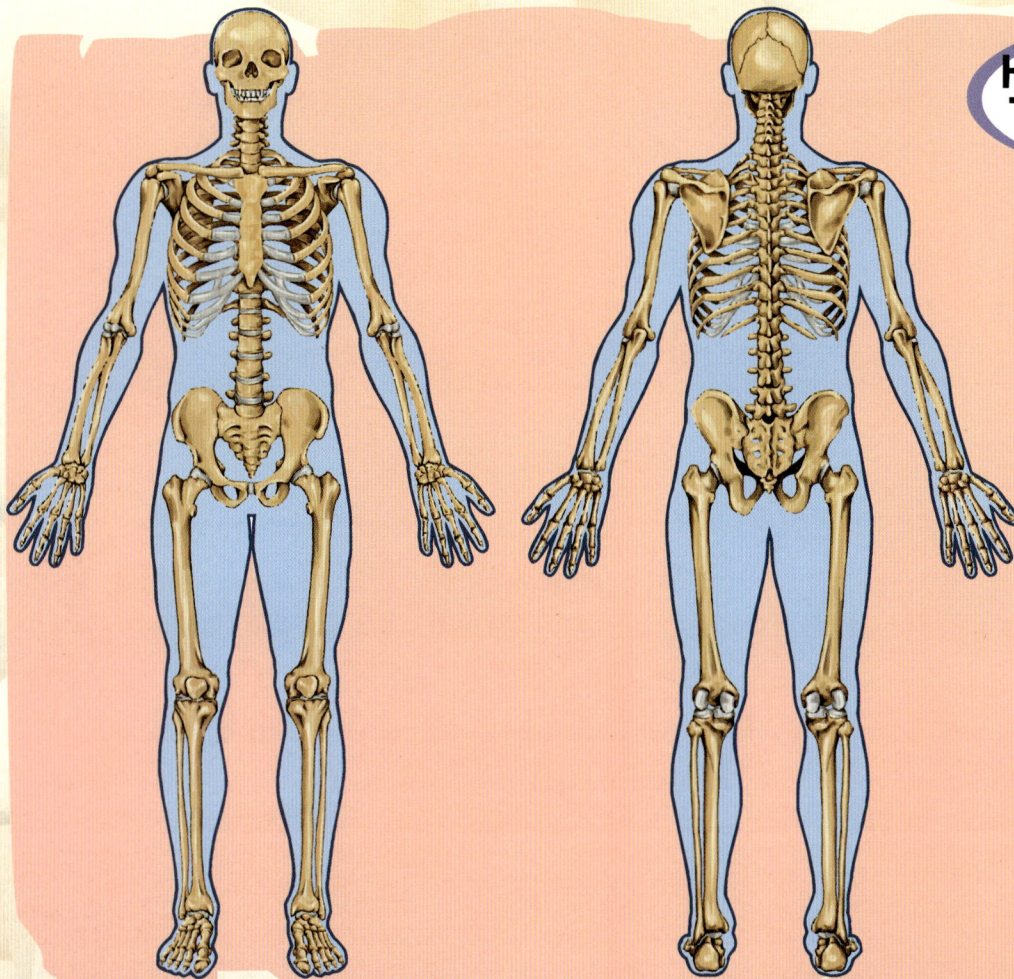

HOW MANY BONES ARE THERE IN THE HUMAN BODY?

When an infant is born, it has 300 bones. Over time, a large number of these bones join together, so that by adulthood, a human being has 206 bones. Around the age of 21, bone mass in the human skeletal framework arrives at its maximum density. Our bones provide our bodies with a supportive frame and protect our organs to an extent.

WHERE ARE THE CARDIAC MUSCLES, AND WHAT IS THEIR FUNCTION?

The heart is mainly made up of muscle. The cells of the cardiac muscle are arranged differently from the other muscles, as the heart has rhythmic contractions since it pumps blood for the body. Factors affecting the cardiac muscle contraction, and the frequency at which it is activated, determine the heart's pumping performance, as well as its response to meet any new demands made by the body.

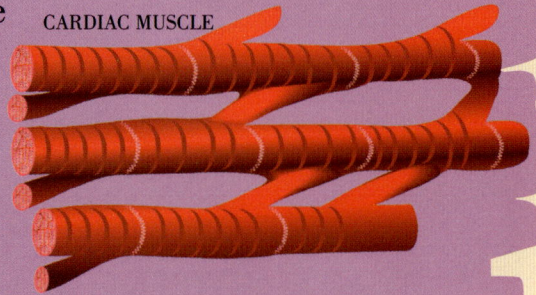

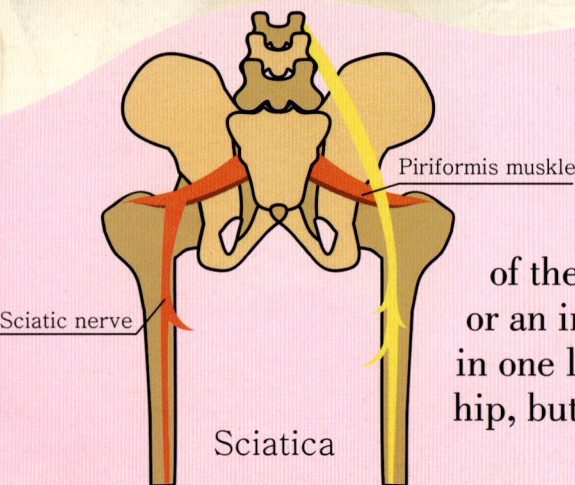

CARDIAC MUSCLE

WHERE IS THE SCIATIC NERVE FOUND?

The sciatic nerve is the body's longest and widest nerve. It goes from the lower spine right down the back of each leg, through the pelvis. It tends to the muscles in the lower leg, which includes the back part of the knee, calf, and ankle. When there is too much pressure or an injury to the sciatic nerve, it typically causes back pain in one leg. The searing pain spreads from the lower back to the hip, buttocks, and leg.

Piriformis muskle

Sciatic nerve

Sciatica

WHAT CHEMICAL IN FOOD CAN CAUSE HIGH BLOOD PRESSURE?

Salt contains sodium, and eating excess salt can lead to high blood pressure or hypertension. Besides, the side effects of certain medications, and the use of illegal drugs, which contain various and harmful chemicals, can also cause secondary hypertension. A severe headache, pounding in the ears or neck, tiredness, vision problems, irregular heartbeat, blood in the urine, or chest pain, are all symptoms of hypertension, in which case one should go to a doctor.

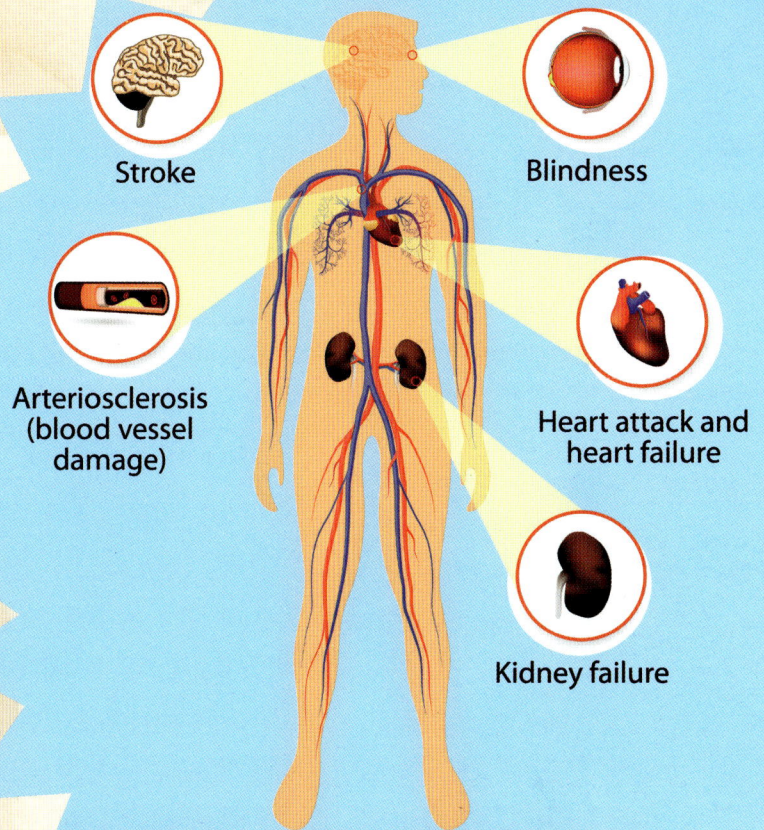

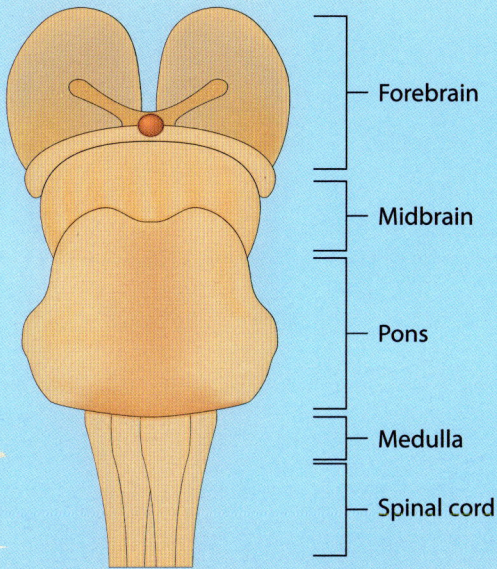

Stroke

Blindness

Arteriosclerosis (blood vessel damage)

Heart attack and heart failure

Kidney failure

Forebrain

Midbrain

Pons

Medulla

Spinal cord

WHICH ACTIONS OF THE BODY ARE CONTROLLED BY THE BRAIN STEM?

The brain stem forms the brain's posterior part and is continuous with the spinal cord. It contains the medulla oblongata, cerebellum, and pons, besides 10 of 12 pairs of cranial nerves. It's a very vital part of the brain, controlling most involuntary actions, such as breathing, heart rate, blood pressure, body temperature, swallowing, and, determines sleepiness and consciousness.

HOW DO THE MOST IMPORTANT MINERALS HELP THE BODY?

There are two types of minerals: macrominerals, which are needed in large amounts, and trace minerals. The most important macrominerals are calcium, iron, potassium, and zinc. Dairy products, salmon, and leafy green vegetables are rich in calcium. Red meat, salmon, eggs, whole grains, and raisins contain a good amount of iron. Bananas, citrus fruits, tomatoes, potatoes, and legumes are rich in potassium. Dark meat, nuts, and legumes have a high amount of zinc.

MAGNESIUM

CALCIUM

FOLATE

POTASSIUM

IRON

SODIUM

FIBER

VITAMIN A

VITAMIN C

WHAT DOES THE WORD, 'SKELETON', MEAN?

The word, 'skeleton', has fairly similar meanings in Latin and Greek. The word, 'sceleton' in modern Latin, means bones, or the bony framework of the body. While the word, 'skeleton', in Greek is a Syriac loan word, used elliptically for skeleton soma, meaning dried-up body, skeleton, or mummy.

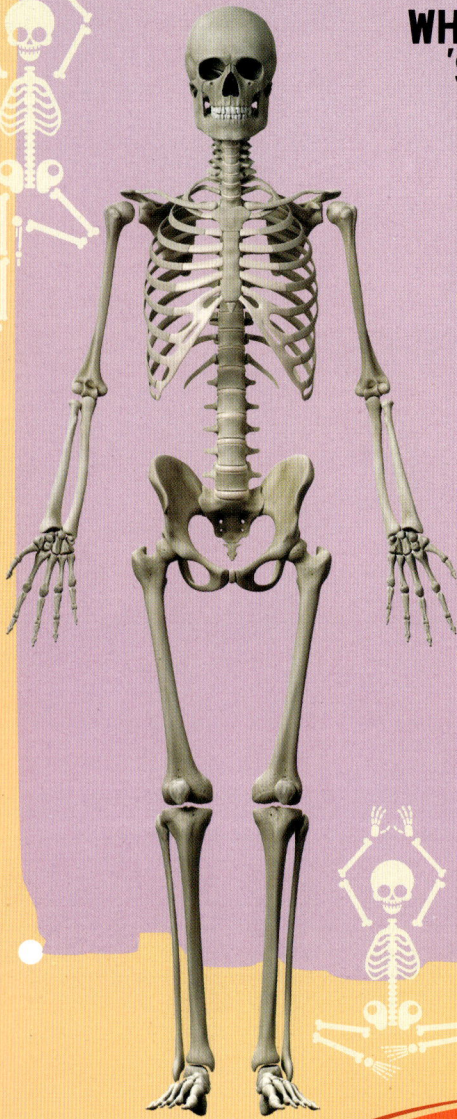

WHICH IS THE SMALLEST ORGAN IN THE HUMAN BODY?

The pineal gland is located close to the brain's centre, between the right and left hemispheres. It's considered to be the human body's smallest organ! The pineal resembles a pine cone and is the smallest endocrine gland. It produces a hormone, melatonin, derived from serotonin, which affects how we sleep, awaken, and respond to seasonal changes. It's also called 'the third eye', has light-sensitive nerve endings, non-visual photoreceptors that react to light, a cornea, and a retina.

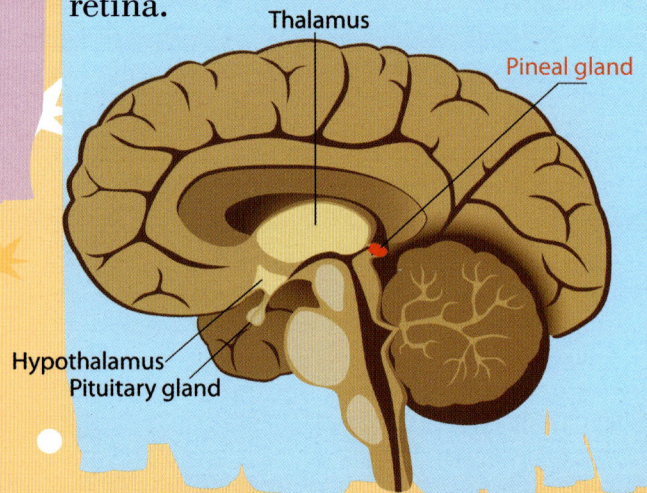

Thalamus
Pineal gland
Hypothalamus
Pituitary gland

WHAT IS THE FUNCTION OF THE SKIN?

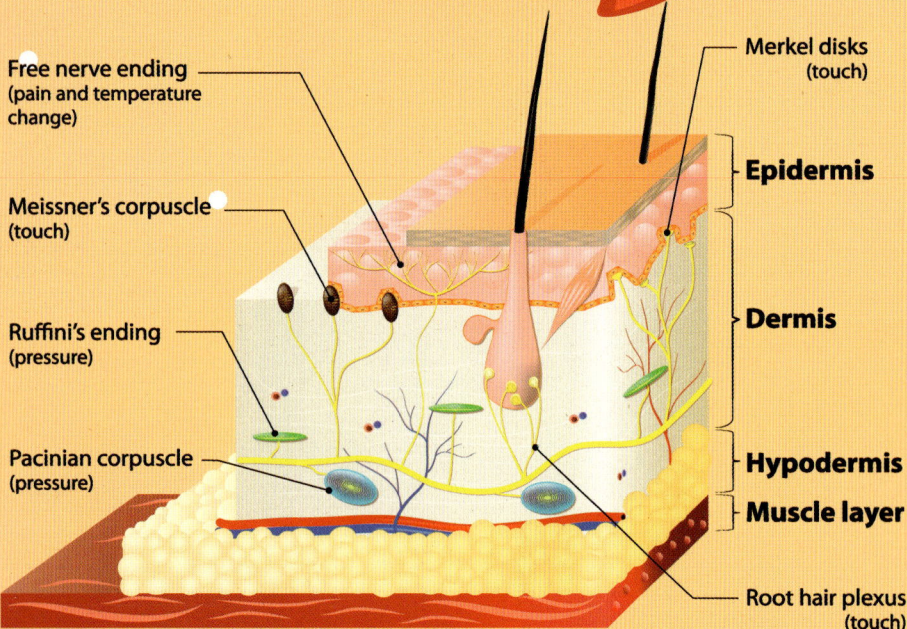

Free nerve ending (pain and temperature change)
Meissner's corpuscle (touch)
Ruffini's ending (pressure)
Pacinian corpuscle (pressure)

Merkel disks (touch)
Epidermis
Dermis
Hypodermis
Muscle layer
Root hair plexus (touch)

The skin's 3 layers: epidermis, dermis, and subcutis or subcutaneous, all help the body in many ways. The skin, though only a few millimetres thick, performs various functions, such as: protecting the body from excessive heat or cold; regulating body temperature; preventing dehydration; producing important hormones; and, storing water and fats.

WHAT DOES THE PULSE RATE INDICATE?

Doctors take the pulse rate by placing a finger over the pulse on the wrist, for one minute. This indicates the expansion and contraction of arteries, in response to the heart's pumping action. For children up to 15 years of age, the normal resting heart rate is between 70-100 beats per minute (bpm); for adults, it's between 60-100 bpm. The pulse rate can reveal heart conditions that need treatment. A very slow rate indicates bradycardia; a very fast rate indicates tachycardia.

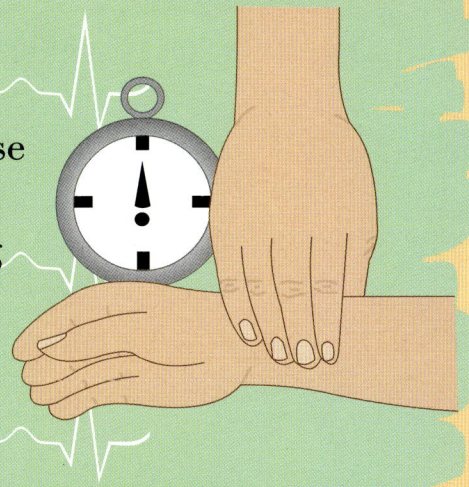

WHAT IS THE SKULL COMPOSED OF?

The human skull, or cranium, is made up of 22 bones, and delicate nervous tissue, with one muscle on the side of the skull. There are 8 cranial bones; and, 14 facial and jawbones. The neurocranium is the cranial cavity, which encircles and protects the brain and brainstem. It contains: the occipital bone, 2 temporal bones, 2 parietal bones, the sphenoid, ethmoid, and frontal bones, all joined together by various sutures. The frontal bone protects the brain's nervous tissue and supports various muscles of the head.

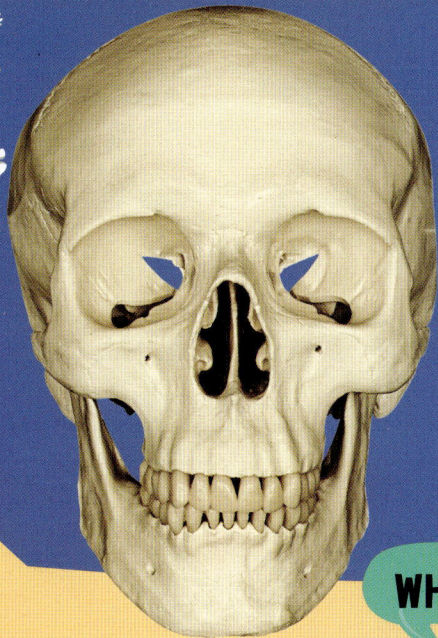

WHAT CAUSES ARTHRITIS?

Any disorder that affects joints, causing pain, stiffness, swelling, and redness, is a cause of arthritis. There are over 100 types of arthritis. The most common is osteoarthritis (OA), rheumatoid arthritis (RA), psoriatic arthritis (PsA), fibromyalgia, gout, and systemic lupus erythematosus (SLE). RA and SLE damage the immune system, needing lifestyle changes. Several forms of arthritis continue throughout life. Vitamin D and omega-3 fatty acids are beneficial in controlling arthritis.

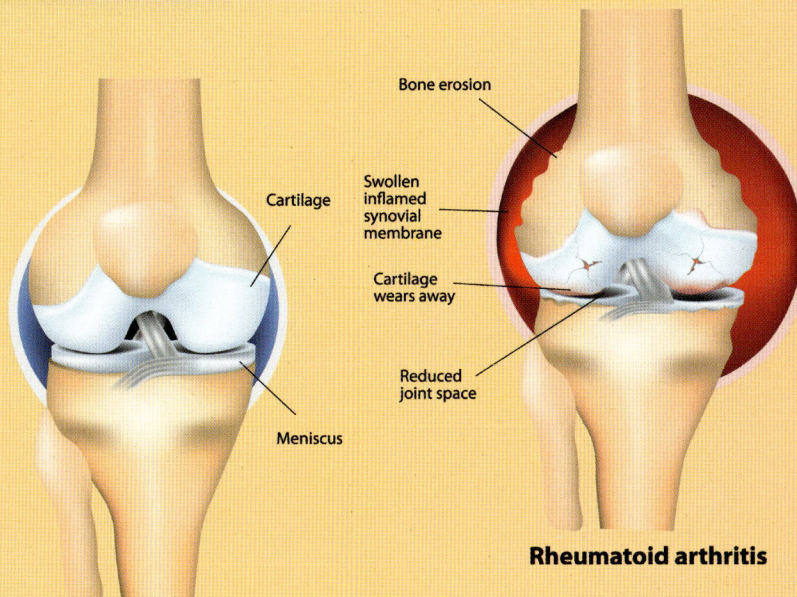

Cartilage

Meniscus

Bone erosion

Swollen inflamed synovial membrane

Cartilage wears away

Reduced joint space

Rheumatoid arthritis

Healthy joint

WHAT IS THE COLOUR OF THE HAIR IF IT CONTAINS CAROTENE?

Beta-carotene is a dark, red-orangish carotenoid pigment, found richly in some fruits and plants. If there is carotene in the hair, its colour will be red. Natural hair colour depends on the melanin pigment made in the hair. Beta-carotene is used in many cosmetics, giving them an orange colour. It restores dry or flaky skin to a smooth and supple one. This organic compound is chemically classified as a hydrocarbon.

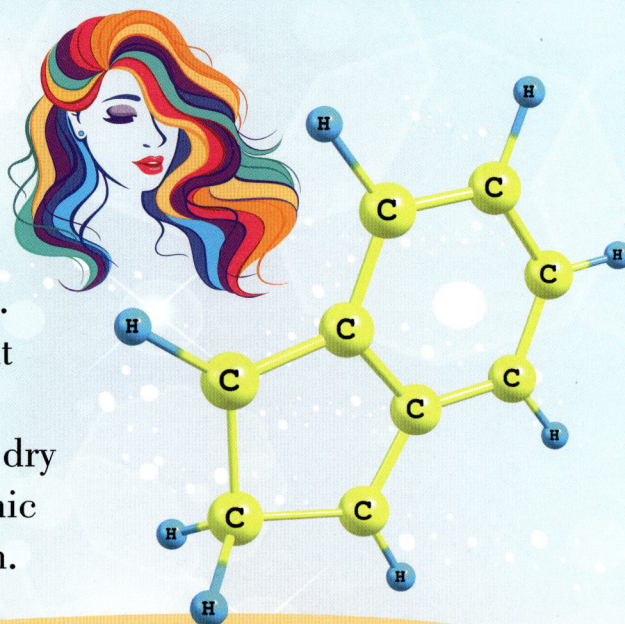

WHAT IS A CONNECTIVE TISSUE COMPOSED OF?

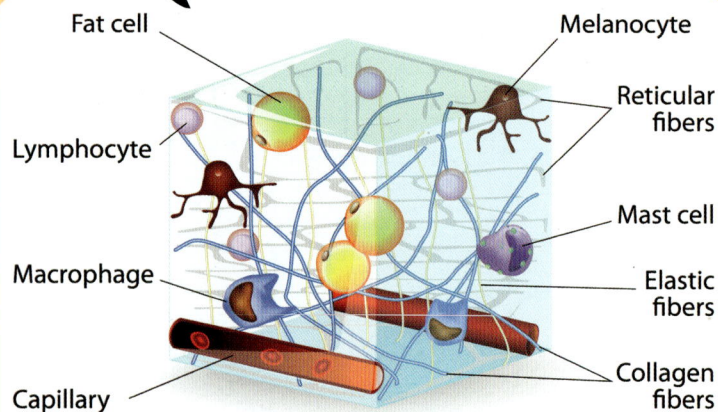

Fat cell
Melanocyte
Reticular fibers
Lymphocyte
Mast cell
Macrophage
Elastic fibers
Collagen fibers
Capillary

The extracellular matrix is made up of a polysaccharide matrix secreted by its cells and protein fibres. Any variation in the extracellular matrix's composition decides the properties of connective tissue. The main types of this tissue are adipose (fat), bone, blood, and cartilage. Connective tissue is also composed of 3 types of fibres, including elastic. Connective tissue binds other tissues, and, maintains the form of the body and organs.

WHAT IS THE HUMAN EYE COMPOSED OF?

Our eye is composed of 3 layers containing various anatomical features. The outermost layer has the cornea and sclera. The middle layer contains the ciliary body, choroid, epithelium, and iris. The retina is in the innermost layer. The spaces of the eye contain aqueous humour, or a clear watery substance, and the vitreous body or jelly-like substance of water and proteins, besides hundreds of fine, transparent fibres.

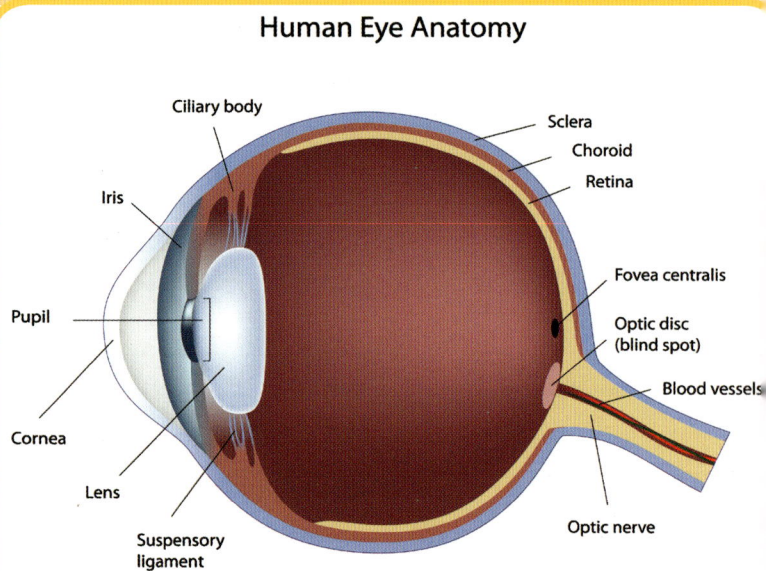

Human Eye Anatomy

Ciliary body
Sclera
Choroid
Retina
Iris
Fovea centralis
Pupil
Optic disc (blind spot)
Blood vessels
Cornea
Lens
Optic nerve
Suspensory ligament

WHAT IS THE SHAPE OF A NORMAL SPINE?

A normal spine has an S-shaped curve, as seen from the side. Its curves help it to withstand a lot of stress, by evenly distributing body weight, to allow flexible movements. It also protects the spinal cord. The neck or cervical spine curves inwards a little, having a backward C-shape, or lordotic curve. Another forward curve is in the low back or lumbar spine. While, the 2 backward curves are made by the chest or thoracic spine, and the hip or sacral spine.

Midline of bladder (over the brachial arterial pulse)

Cuff (containing inflatable rubber bladder)

Lower edge of cuff (2–3cm above the antecubital fossa)

Automated sphygmomanometer

Antecubital fossa

127
83
70

Bladder

Midline of bladder

40% of arm circumference

80% of arm circumference

WHERE IS THE RADIAL PULSE?

The radial pulse is located on the wrist. The radial artery is an extension of the brachial artery, coming down from the forearm to the wrist, where it rises slightly and is closest to the surface near the thumb. This artery supplies oxygenated blood to the arm and hand and is most commonly used to check the pulse rate at the left or right wrist.

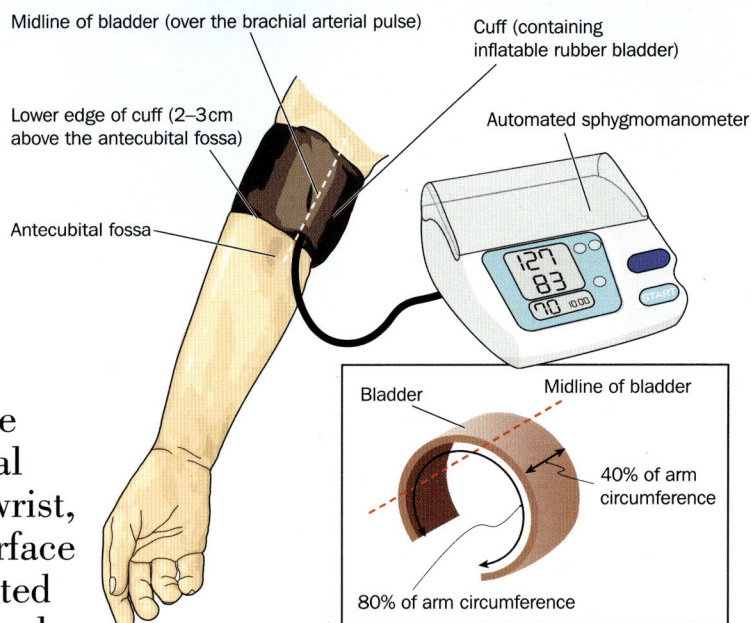

WHAT IS ALOPECIA?

Alopecia, or hair loss, can be a permanent or temporary feature. Even women experience this condition, but it's more pronounced in men. In androgenetic alopecia, androgens or male hormones combine with genetic factors, to cause gradual hair loss. In alopecia areata, a person has patches of baldness where the hair grows back. In traction alopecia, the hair thins due to making tight braids; while, in telogen effluvium, people lose hair due to sudden weight loss, fever, or after childbirth.

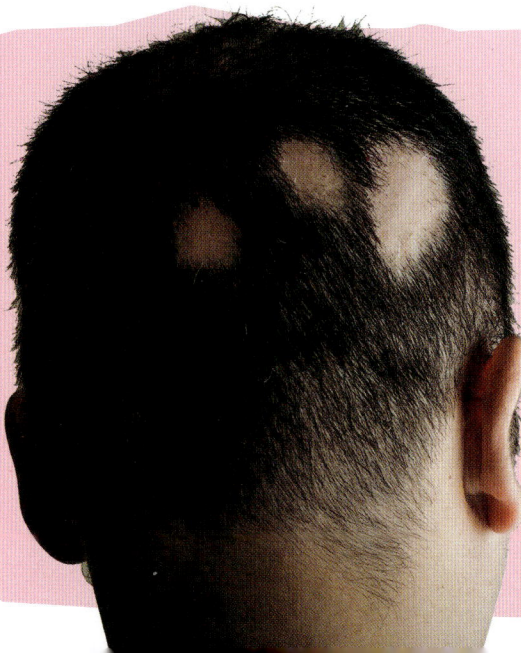

WHY ARE TEARS SALTY?

The commonest salt found in bodily fluids is table salt, or sodium chloride (NaCl). On average, a little above 6mg of dissolved NaCl is present in 1ml of lacrimal fluid or tear fluid, in the human body. This is what makes tears taste salty, just like sweat. All tears flow out of tear glands, beneath the upper eyelids. They get drained out of the two tear ducts, with one located close to the inside corner in each eye.

HOW DOES THE COLOUR OF THE EYE DEVELOP?

The iris of the eye contains pigmentation that gives it its colour. A baby's eye colour is determined by genes it inherits from its' parents, which account for: brown, green, and blue colours. How eyes become grey, hazel, or have other combinations, is not yet fully clear. In some children, blue eyes darken within the first 3 years, as melanin, a brown pigment, develops with age!

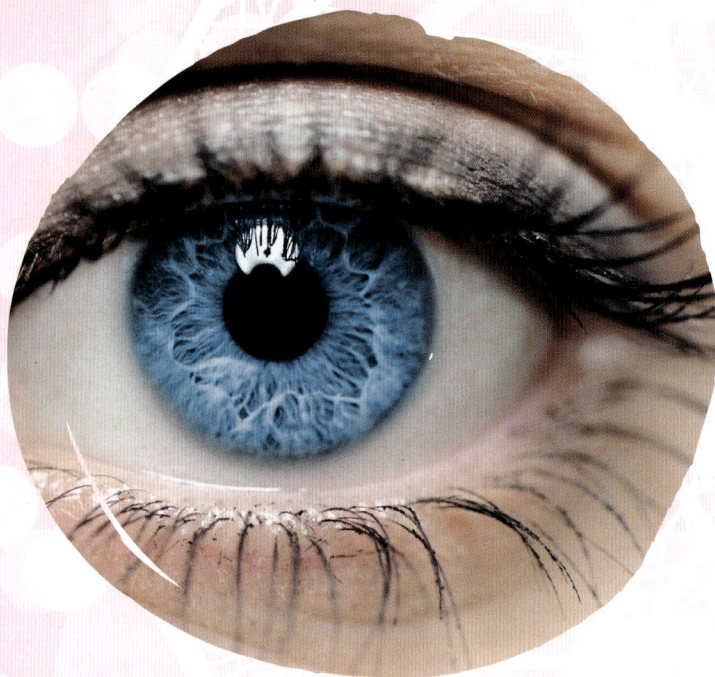

WHICH PART OF OUR BODY IS LEAST SENSITIVE TO TOUCH?

Tiny cells in our skin, called receptors or sensory neurons, send a signal to the brain as soon as we touch anything, and the brain at once makes us realize whether we have touched something hot, cold, rough, frizzy, etc. Pain levels and tolerance vary in different people. But some parts of the body are very sensitive to touch, while others are not. Among the least sensitive body areas are the shoulder, outer arm, buttocks, and calf.

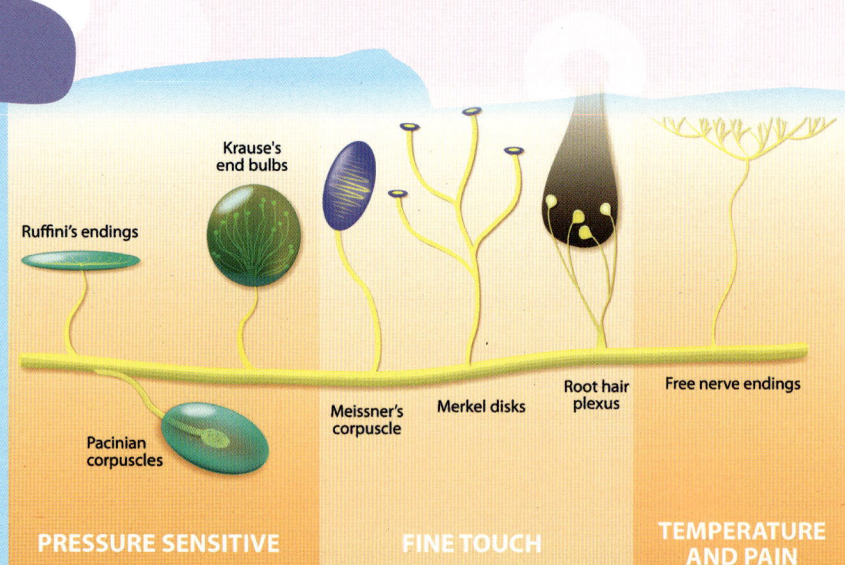

Ruffini's endings
Krause's end bulbs
Pacinian corpuscles
Meissner's corpuscle
Merkel disks
Root hair plexus
Free nerve endings

PRESSURE SENSITIVE   **FINE TOUCH**   **TEMPERATURE AND PAIN**

WHAT IS THE TONGUE MADE OF?

The tongue is a muscular organ, covered with pink, moist tissue or mucosa. Tiny bumps on the tongue give it a rough texture. These are called papillae, which are covered by thousands of taste buds. There are mucous and serous glands beneath the papillae, besides a layer each of skeletal muscle and connective tissue, and pockets of adipose (fat). It's the skeletal muscle that enables the movement of the tongue.

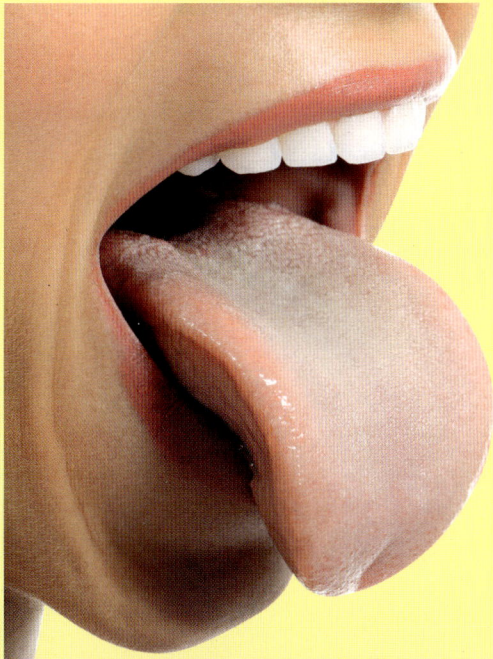

WHAT IS HYPOXEMIA?

Hypoxemia is an abnormal oxygen deficiency in arterial blood, often caused by respiratory disorders when the blood cannot supply sufficient oxygen to the body and can lead to hypoxia. Extreme hypoxemia is called anoxemia. Suffocation, or obstructive sleep apnea; muscle weakness; or, structural deformities of the chest, are some of the conditions that restrict airflow and cause hypoxemia.

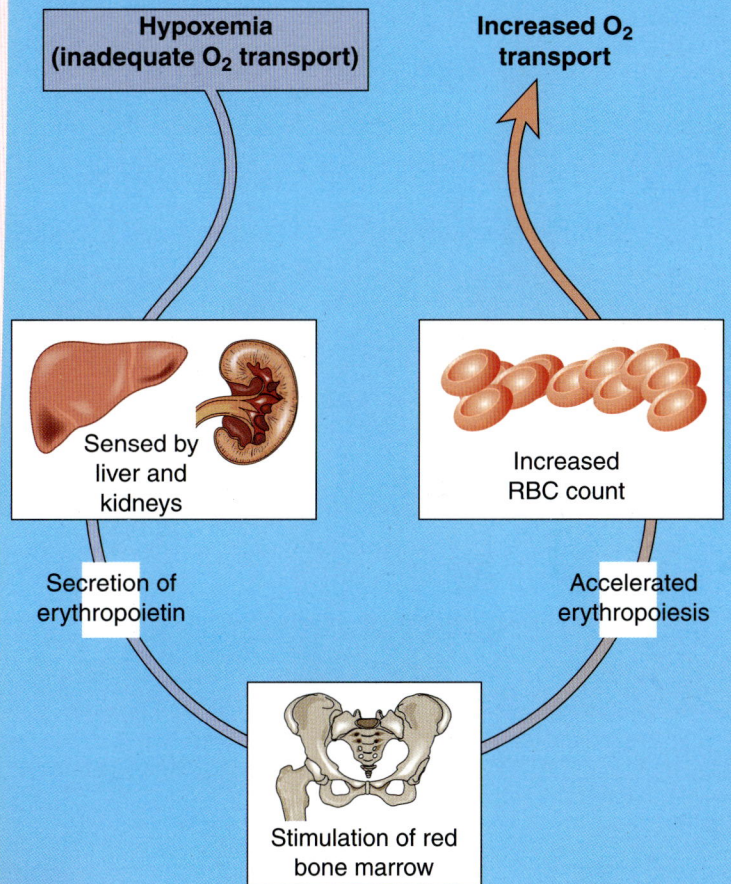

Hypoxemia (inadequate O_2 transport)

Increased O_2 transport

Sensed by liver and kidneys

Increased RBC count

Secretion of erythropoietin

Accelerated erythropoiesis

Stimulation of red bone marrow

WHICH PART OF THE BODY HAS A 'DRUM', AND WHAT ARE ITS OTHER PARTS?

The only part of the body with a 'drum', is the ear! It has an eardrum. The different parts of the ear are the pinna or the ear flap; the eardrum or tympanic membrane, dividing the external ear from the middle ear; the tympanic cavity or middle ear, consisting of the ossicles, or the ear's 3 tiny bones; and, the inner ear, which has the cochlea.

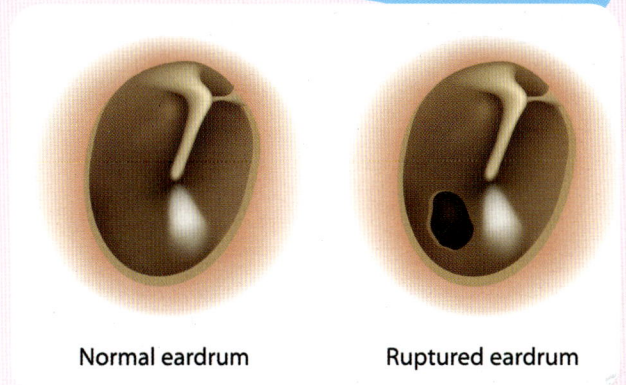

Normal eardrum

Ruptured eardrum

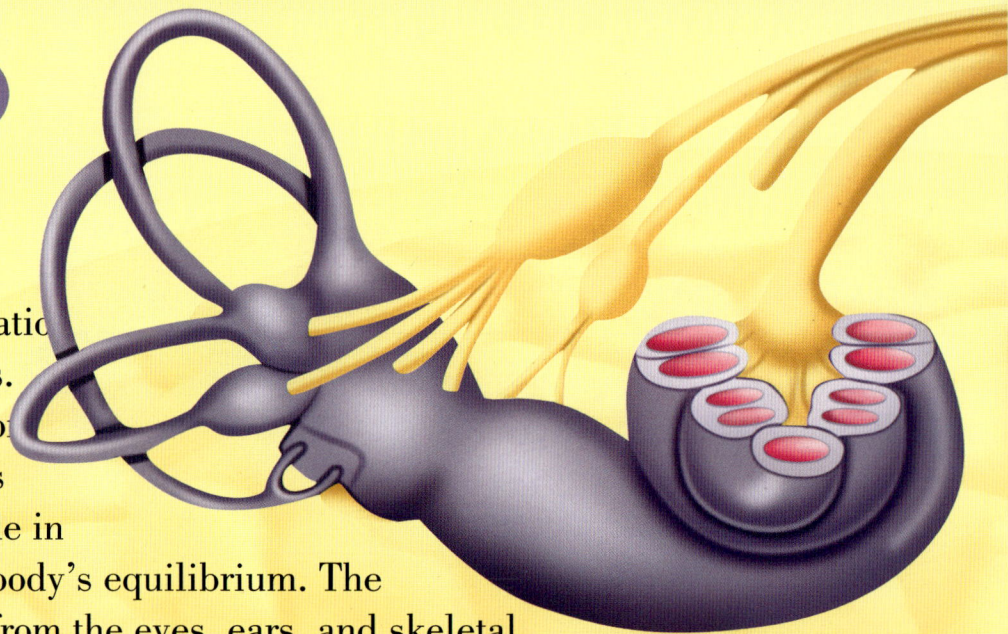

Our senses of sight and hearing work in coordination with body muscles and joints. The cochlea is responsible for our sense of hearing; besides which, the utricle and saccule in the ear, help in keeping the body's equilibrium. The brain responds to messages from the eyes, ears, and skeletal system, to control movement and coordination, keep balance, and perform various activities skilfully.

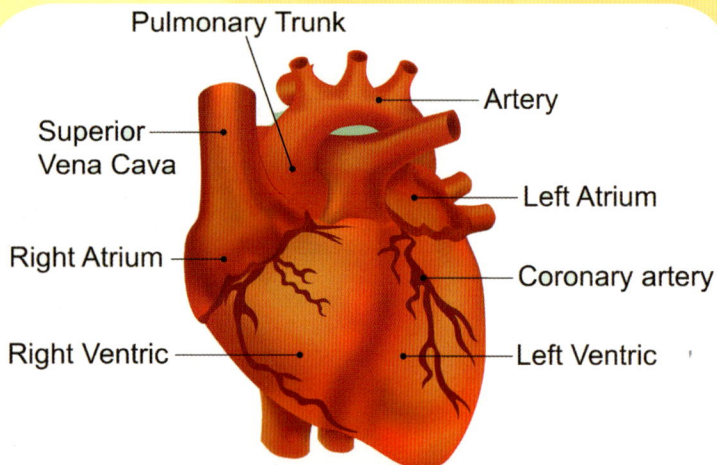

- Pulmonary Trunk
- Superior Vena Cava
- Artery
- Left Atrium
- Right Atrium
- Coronary artery
- Right Ventric
- Left Ventric

WHAT HAPPENS WHEN A PERSON GETS CONJUNCTIVITIS?

Conjunctivitis, also called 'pink eye', causes infection or inflammation of the conjunctiva, lining the eyelid, and covering the white part of the eyeball. The tiny blood vessels of the conjunctiva make the eyes appear pink or reddish when inflamed. It can be caused due to numerous reasons, such as viruses, bacteria, allergens, chemicals, fungi, amoeba or parasites, and, air pollution. Both, viral and bacterial conjunctivitis are highly infectious.

WHERE IS THE VENA CAVA VEIN, AND WHAT DOES IT DO?

Humans have 2 vena cava veins: the superior vena cava, and the inferior vena cava, both of which empty into the heart's right atrium. The inferior vena cava runs behind the abdominal cavity, and along the spine's right vertebral column. It's the biggest vein in our bodies and carries blood from the body's lower part, travelling up, along the abdominal aorta.

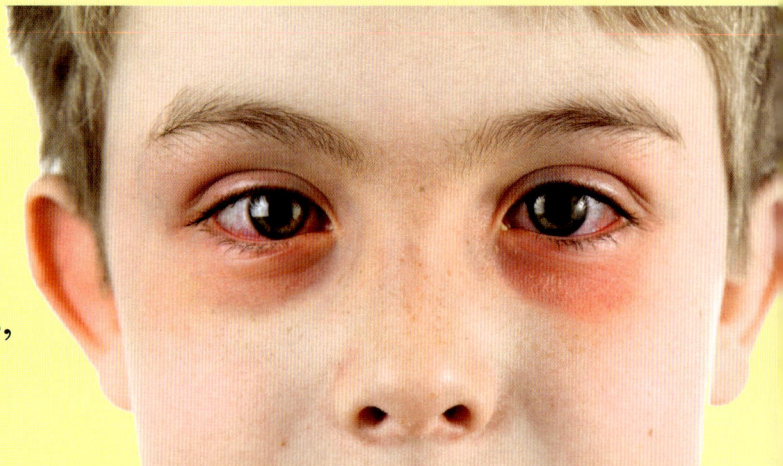

WHAT IS BILE AND WHERE IS IT PRODUCED IN THE BODY?

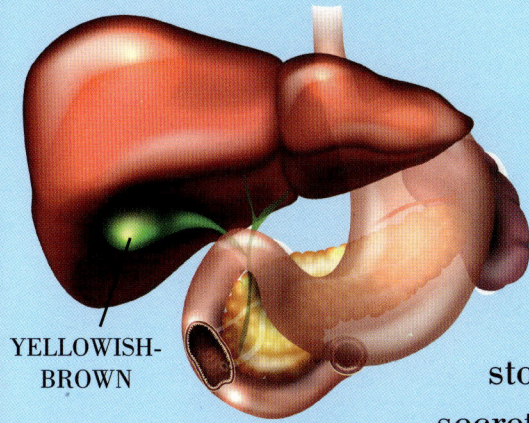

Bile, dark green to the yellowish-brown fluid that contains acids, is produced by the liver and is critical for the digestion of lipids in the small intestine. It's constantly produced by the liver, in humans, and stored in the gallbladder. Many of the body's waste is secreted into the bile and eliminated in faeces. At times, people may suffer from bile reflux, for which experts suggest that one should stop smoking, limit or avoid alcohol, limit fatty foods, sit upright after eating, and relax.

YELLOWISH-BROWN

WHICH PART OF THE BODY CAN SUNLIGHT DAMAGE?

First of all, it's the skin that is at risk of damage by sunlight. Even the melanin, in the skin, can't prevent the entire damage. Sunlight makes vitamin D for us, but over-exposure to the sun brings unpleasant results, like sunburn, skin aging, eye or skin damage, heatstroke, and, worst of all, skin cancer. The risk in people with lighter skin is higher for skin damage and skin cancer!

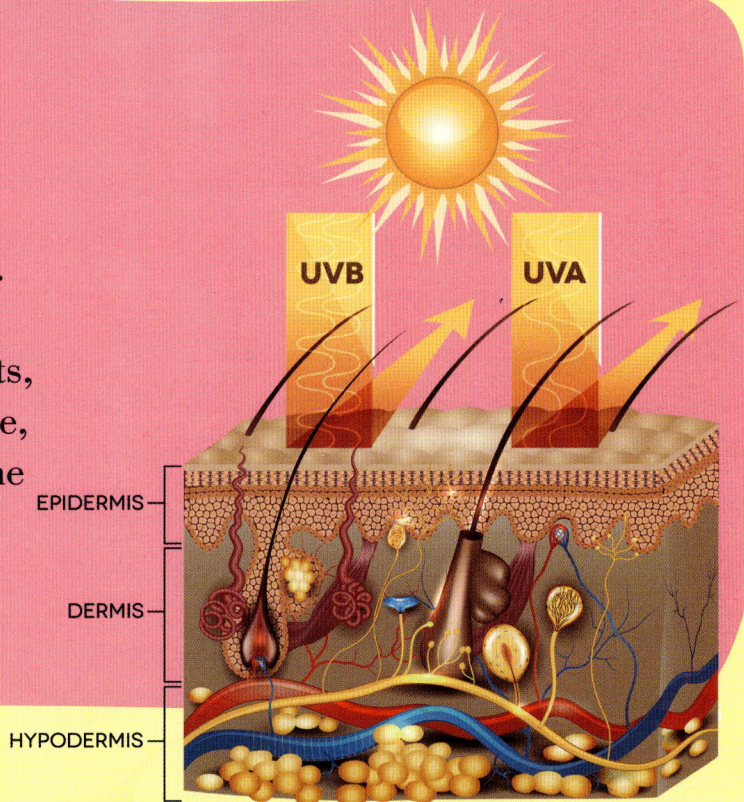

UVB   UVA

EPIDERMIS

DERMIS

HYPODERMIS

IS THERE ANY FACTOR THAT DETERMINES OUR HEIGHT?

It's believed that genes account for 60%-80% of a person's final height. For the remaining, there are a few other factors that can contribute to height, including exercise, and nutrition. Eating a nutritious diet, and the right amount of food, through childhood and adolescence, can help to increase one's height.

HOW LOUD IS A WHISPER IN DECIBELS?

A whisper is said to have a sound intensity of about 20-30 decibels (dB), and normal speech is around 50 dB. The sound of bird calls is said to have a sound intensity of around 44 dB, while traffic in a busy city, can be roughly about 85 dB. If one is exposed to the sound intensity of 85 dB over a long period of time, it can ultimately cause hearing damage. And is there anything softer than a whisper? Yes. It's breathing, which is barely audible at 10 dB!

WHY ARE CARBOHYDRATES IMPORTANT FOR US?

Our body uses foods containing carbohydrates to make glucose, a sort of sugar, which can be immediately used as energy, or stored for later use. Carbohydrates also use most of the protein we consume for tissue synthesis, like the building up of muscles. They prevent degradation of skeletal muscle and other tissues including the heart, liver, and kidneys; help with fat metabolism; and, are a rich source of many vitamins and minerals. Foods like grains, cereals, bread, peas, potatoes, and bananas are rich in carbohydrates.

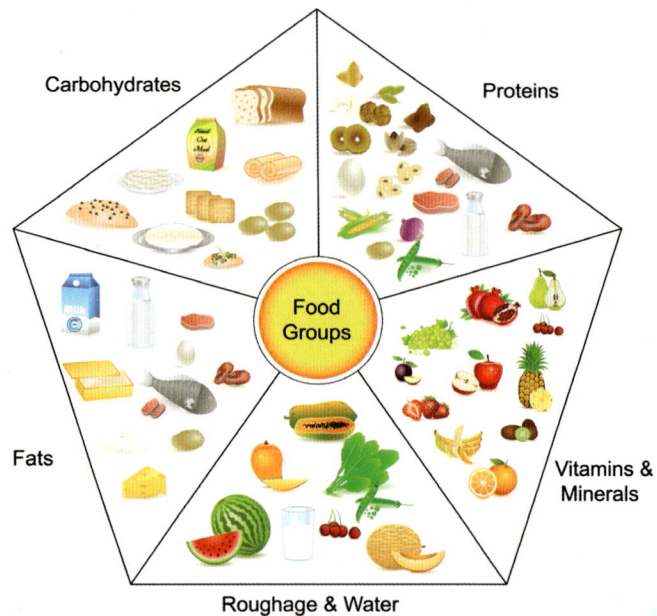

HOW DO VITAMINS HELP US?

Our body needs 13 essential vitamins, of which 4: A, D, E, and K are fat-soluble, while the remainder are water-soluble. Some are antioxidants; play a vital role in the metabolism of proteins and carbohydrates; formation of red blood cells, hormones, and cholesterol; blood coagulation; or, maintain healthy skin and nerves. These are found in fruits, vegetables, whole grains, fortified dairy products, beans, and lentils. Besides, multivitamins are taken orally, which contain various vitamins and minerals.

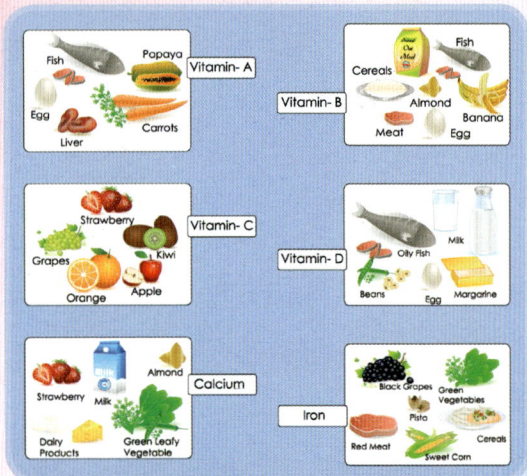

WHAT IS AN OPAQUE CORNEA?

The cornea is the clear, outermost part of the eye, helping to focus vision. Tears nourish and protect it. An opaque cornea is a cloudy cornea.

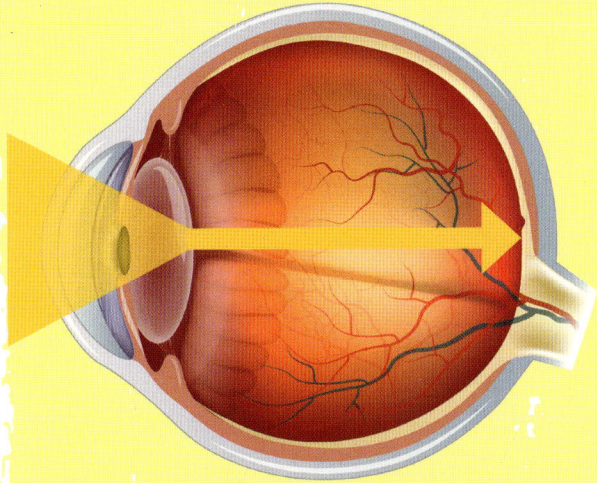

When there is a build-up of material clouding the cornea, it leads to sight impairment. It may be there by birth or acquired due to various reasons, including infection, inflammation, injury, dry eyes, keratitis, or trachoma, causing differing amounts of vision loss.

WHAT ROLE DOES MAGNESIUM PLAY IN OUR BODY?

Magnesium assists our body in over 300 biochemical reactions. It helps in keeping a healthy immune system, keeps the heartbeat steady, maintains normal muscle and nerve functions, and helps bones to remain strong. Besides, it helps in regulating blood glucose levels, creating protein and energy, and lowering blood pressure in hypertension. Lack of magnesium is believed to cause depression and frequent migraines. Pumpkin seeds, boiled spinach, dark chocolate, black beans, halibut, mackerel, salmon, avocados, almonds, and cashews are excellent sources of magnesium.

HOW MANY VERTEBRAE ARE THERE IN THE BACKBONE?

In humans, the vertebral or spinal column, also called the backbone or spine, mostly consists of 33 vertebrae. There are 24 presacral vertebrae, including 7 cervical, 12 thoracic, and 5 lumbar; the sacrum has 5 fused sacral vertebrae; while the coccyx has 4 mostly fused coccygeal vertebrae. The chief function of the vertebral column is to safeguard the spinal cord, besides helping us to walk or stand.

IF A PERSON SUFFERS FROM DIARRHOEA, WHAT CAN BE GIVEN FOR QUICK RELIEF?

There are over-the-counter (OTC) medicines that deal with diarrhoea. Experts advise plenty of clear liquids, and water should be had for the first 24 hours. Gradually, the BRAT diet can be added: Bananas, Rice, Applesauce, and Toast. Milk and alcohol should be avoided. Fruit juice without pulp, soda without caffeine, chicken broth without fat, tea with honey, and sports drinks are recommended. Bananas are particularly helpful as they make up the potassium lost through diarrhoea.

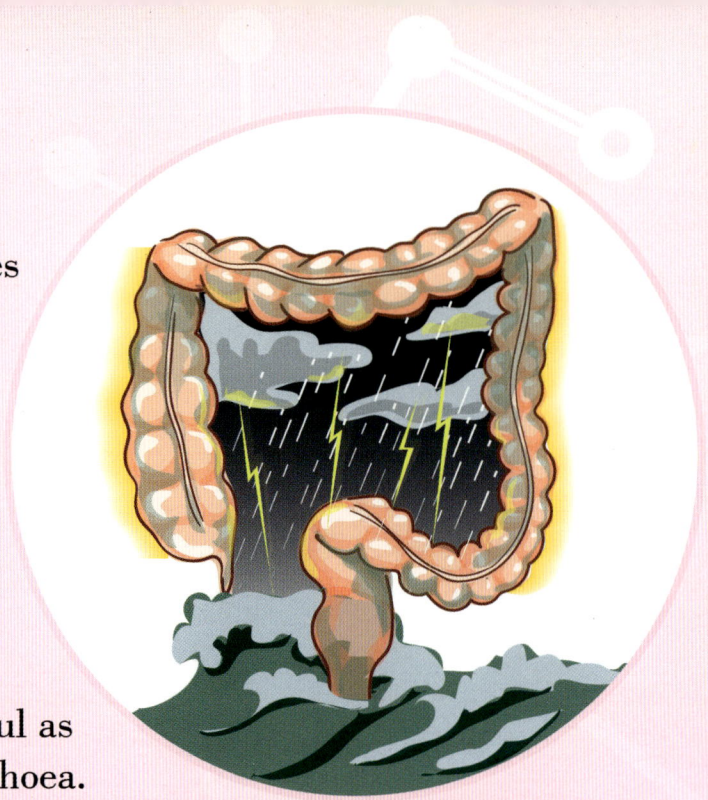

WHAT CAN AN IRREGULARITY IN CHROMOSOMES LEAD TO?

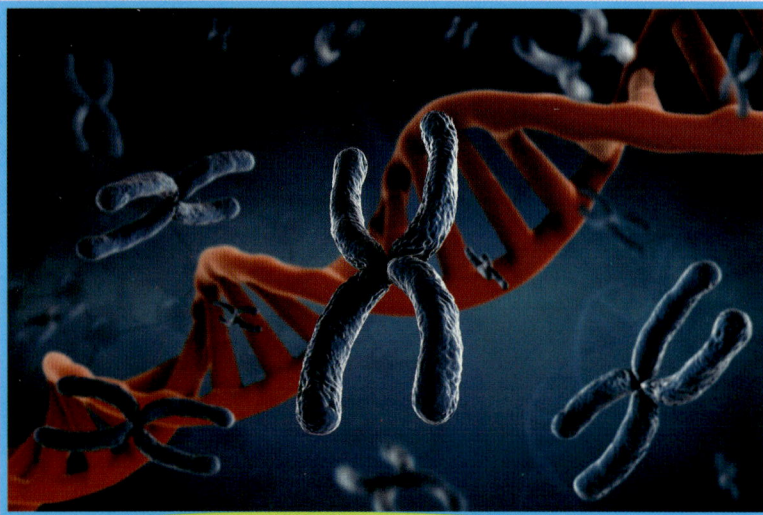

Every chromosome contains thousands of genes needed to make proteins, which help in growth, development, and chemical reactions. At times, abnormalities occur, which may be due to an error in cell division, while some conditions are not inherited. Seizures, learning disabilities, mild to severe levels of mental retardation, certain heart, and circulatory problems, are all due to an irregularity in chromosomes.

WHAT ARE THE SYMPTOMS AND CAUSES OF DIZZINESS?

Dizziness causes an immediate sense of feeling unsteady, lightheaded, or loss of balance. If the dizziness persists, a person may faint. There are many causes of dizziness, which include disturbances of vision, the inner ear, brain, or the gastrointestinal system; getting hit on the side of the head or the ear; having a migraine, too much alcohol, or as a side effect of medications.

HOW IMPORTANT IS VACCINATION, AND DOES IT ALWAYS WORK?

Vaccination helps to prevent the onset of many diseases, and some shots are given from birth for measles, mumps, hepatitis B, diphtheria, tetanus, tuberculosis, and yellow fever. Most are for viral infections, with some are for bacterial as well, and booster doses are given to children to combat certain infections. Polio has been eradicated. But, no fully effective vaccines presently exist to fight leprosy, pneumonic plague, or typhoid.

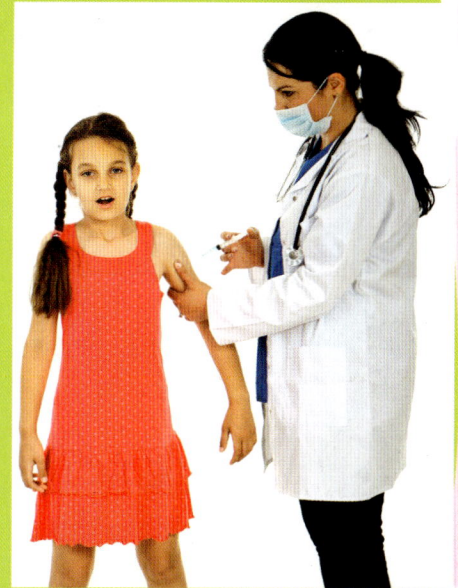

WHAT HELPS TO HEAL DAMAGED TISSUE?

CONNECTIVE TISSUES

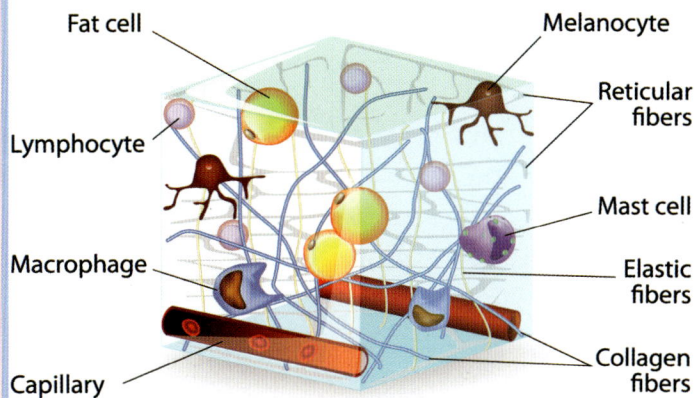

Fat cell
Melanocyte
Lymphocyte
Reticular fibers
Mast cell
Macrophage
Elastic fibers
Collagen fibers
Capillary

The healing of damaged tissue involves regeneration or replacement. In regeneration, portions of damaged tissue can be fully restored to its original state. When tissue gets severely damaged or is unable to heal on its own, it has to be replaced with connective tissue. Most soft-tissue injuries affect muscles, tendons, or ligaments in the body, causing bruising, pain, swelling, and loss of function. Mild muscular strains can heal on their own, but severe strains require surgery or are put into a cast for several weeks.

WHAT ARE MOVEMENT DISORDERS?

A neurological condition that causes abnormal, increased movements, is a movement disorder. The movements may be voluntary, or involuntary, but they affect the speed, ease, and fluency of movements, and are movements over which the affected person has no control. Such disorders include ataxia, athetosis, chorea, dystonia, functional movement disorder, multiple system atrophy, Parkinson's disease, Parkinsonism, restless legs syndrome, Wilson's disease, tremor, etc.

Index